WHERE DO I START?

Your Essential
Gluten-Free, Dairy-Free and Sugar-Free

FOOD ALLERGY
Cookbook

Victoria Yeh

Foreword by Dr. Meghan Walker, N.D.

Vector One Publishing
Toronto, Ontario, Canada

Published by Vector One Publishing, Toronto, Ontario, Canada.
First edition

National Library of Canada Cataloguing-in-Publication Data
Yeh, Victoria, 1981-
    Where do I start? : your essential gluten-free, dairy-free and sugar-free food allergy cookbook / Victoria Yeh ; foreword by Meghan Walker. -- 1st ed.

Includes bibliographical references and index.
ISBN 978-0-9864811-0-9

    1. Gluten-free diet--Recipes. 2. Milk-free diet--Recipes. 3. Sugar-free diet--Recipes. I. Title.

RM237.86.Y33 2010   641.5'6318   C2009-907437-0

Printed in Canada

Visit us online at www.GlutenFreeLiving.ca

DEDICATION

This book is dedicated to everyone who has ever felt frustration, anxiety, despair or sadness because of their food intolerances. I hope this book empowers you with the knowledge and confidence to embrace and enjoy your new lifestyle. This book is meant to give you basic knowledge and tools that you can apply to your everyday life in order to successfully adapt to your specific dietary needs. I hope that this book helps you achieve greater health, energy and happiness.

Thank you to my family for supporting me throughout the years. I especially want to thank my husband, Trevor, for helping me stay on track everyday and for his constant encouragement and love.

ACKNOWLEDGEMENTS

I would like to thank some of the health care providers who have been pivotal in my journey to achieve superior health, including my great aunt and talented acupuncturist, Lili Jiang (Winnipeg, MN), Dr. John Gannage (Markham, ON), Dr. Harald Rosenfeld (Thamesford, ON) and Dr. Derek Lee (Unionville, ON).

I also wish to express special gratitude to Dr. Meghan Walker from the Integrative Health Institute (Toronto, ON) for her feedback and contributions to this project.

ABOUT THE AUTHOR

Victoria Yeh is a Toronto based author, musician and owner of Gluten-Free Toronto. For over eight years, she has lived with and successfully adapted to multiple food intolerances to wheat, gluten, dairy, soy, sugar, corn and yeast. With the launch of her new book, website, blog, and seminars, Victoria is setting out to help educate others on how to adapt to their unique dietary needs and achieve their goals for greater long-term health.

TABLE OF CONTENTS

FOREWORD..1

CHAPTER 1: THE STRUGGLE..3

A PERSONAL JOURNEY 3
WHAT AM I GOING TO EAT?..4
KNOWLEDGE IS POWER 5

CHAPTER 2: INSIDE THE KITCHEN 7

FOOD SAFETY..7
   Cross Contamination 7
   Buyer Beware 9
   Basic Food Safety..10
   Fire Safety 12
TOOLS OF THE TRADE..12
   Keeping Your Inventory – Filling Your Pantry............................12
   Equipment...13
BEING EFFICIENT WITH YOUR TIME..16
   Buying in Bulk 16
   Storing in Bulk..17
   Cooking Meals For a Family With a Variety of Needs 18
SUMMARY..18

CHAPTER 3: MAKING SUCCESSFUL SUBSTITUTIONS 19

SUBSTITUTIONS 19
GLUTEN AND WHEAT 20
   Substituting For Wheat And Gluten 23
   Wheat Flour as Bulk..23
   Gluten as a Binding (Sticky) Aid 23
   Gluten as a Leavening (Rising) Aid 26
   Substitution Examples..27
DAIRY...30
   Substitutions 31
   Substitution Example 34
SUGAR 35
   Substitutions 36
   Substitution Example 38
SOY 40
   Substitutions 41

Corn 42
    Substitutions 43
Troubleshooting Guide 44

CHAPTER 4: ENJOY A VARIETY OF FOODS 47

Grains 47
Vegetables 48
    Leafy And Salad Vegetables 49
    Fruits (Excluding Squashes and Melons) 53
    Squashes And Melons 54
    Flowers And Flower Buds 55
    Podded Vegetables 55
    Root And Tuberous Vegetables 58
Meats 62

CLOSING REMARKS 65

CHAPTER 5: RECIPES 67

Soups 67
Breakfast 77
Vegetables 91
Wraps and Sandwiches 109
Entrées 115
Snacks and Deserts 145

COOKING CONVERSIONS 163

BIBLIOGRAPHY 169

INDEX 173

FOREWORD

The incidence of Celiac disease is estimated to affect 1% of the population and that number is continuing to grow. Clinically, 75% of my patients either report having a sensitivity to the foods they are eating or discover that their symptoms can be resolved by removing strategic elements in their diet. The diagnosis of food sensitivities, including Celiac disease, has been commonly associated with significant digestive symptoms, yet in reality, only 35% of newly diagnosed Celiac cases actually report having any diarrhea. For most people, even doctors, what we eat is rarely considered as the primary cause of chronic physical complaints, yet seemingly normal symptoms such as post-nasal drip, leg cramps, heartburn and eczema have all been linked to food sensitivities for some people.

Food is not what it used to be. Processing, cross-contamination and in some cases, entirely manmade consumable products have filled the landscape of North American grocery stores resulting in calorie-rich, nutrient-poor selections. Given this environment it should be no surprise that some of our bodies lack the capacity to effectively process such a rapidly evolving selection of food.

For most of my patients, the biggest challenge of dealing with food sensitivities are not the symptoms themselves, but learning to prepare meals that satisfy the void that had previously been filled with bagels and freshly baked bread. Food is such a powerful mediator of the experiences in our lives that when we are suddenly "denied" the things that have previously provided comfort and tradition, we feel as though life will never be the same. When it comes to the enjoyment of what we eat however, this does not have to be the case. Creative gluten-free flour combinations, strategic dairy substitutions and informed sugar alternatives mean that you can enjoy baking and cooking without suffering from the inevitable discomforts that arise following the consumption of ingredients to which we are sensitive.

In *Where Do I Start?* Victoria provides concise and user-friendly information about how to substitute glutinous flours with flavourful and texture-conscious alternatives. While many gluten-free cookbooks list one or two options for regular wheat flour, Victoria provides background information on the healthy flour, dairy and sugar options that will not only allow you to succeed in adopting new recipes, but an entirely new lifestyle as well.

My personal journey with Celiac disease began like many others; it was discovered by accident. I carried a series of symptoms that followed me throughout my childhood and into my life as a young adult. I never sought assistance, because like many people, I had always assumed they were something everyone experienced. It was not until I began my training as a Naturopathic Doctor that I discovered the dramatic connection between what I eat and the way I feel. It has taken a great deal of time and investigation to learn the ins and outs of a gluten-free lifestyle and I am still learning as I go. What took me years of research has been surpassed in this book. *Where Do I Start?* takes the time and effort of tedious online investigations and packs it together into a definitive resource that will inevitably become a "go-to" guide for anyone challenged with a sensitivity to the things they eat.

Meghan Walker
Naturopathic Doctor

CHAPTER 1:
THE STRUGGLE

A PERSONAL JOURNEY

As a kid growing up in the suburbs of Ottawa, I had a pretty typical childhood. I had mild chicken pox as a baby, the odd ear infection and stomach ache, and of course scraped up my knees once in a while playing outside with my friends. As I grew older, though, ear and throat infections became more regular, and I began to complain of nausea, dizziness, headaches and abdominal discomfort. My parents dutifully took me to doctors, who would either give me antibiotics, painkillers or simply dismiss my complaints. But at no point did anyone consider the possibility that everything was related to what I was eating. (Well, I was perceptive enough to know that eating three cream-filled doughnuts in one sitting gave me stomach aches!) The only obvious sign I had to the real cause of my problems appeared when, at age 10, I broke out in total body hives after eating a sugary fruit compote. An allergist later revealed that I was allergic to pesticides. So, for over a decade following that very itchy experience, I avoided most berries until organic ones became widely available.

While I did have several other food sensitivities, they remained almost completely unrecognized until my early 20s when I visited an M.D. who was practicing integrative and holistic medicine. By this time, I had been searching for years for relief from what had become frequent nausea, motion sickness, abdominal discomfort, and recurrent throat infections. Even though I was otherwise very healthy, fit and active, I knew that something just wasn't quite right, and that there had to be a solution out there aside from prescription drugs. Fortunately, through my new doctor, I finally came to realize that all my symptoms were in fact related, that I didn't have to accept feeling less than 100% everyday, and that contrary to previous opinions, it wasn't "all in my head." My new doctor helped me develop the strong belief that nutrition is truly the fundamental basis to achieving and maintaining overall good health. And even more importantly – knowing what nutrition is specifically right for *each* individual.

WHAT AM I GOING TO EAT?

At my very first appointment, my doctor told me to eliminate wheat, dairy and sugar from my diet. (He also forbade caffeine and alcohol, but luckily I never drank either in the first place.) Later tests would also reveal sensitivities to peppers, tomatoes, potatoes, eggplant, corn, soy, pork, beef and yeast. Yikes! All I could see was a huge list of food that I couldn't eat. For weeks, I literally wandered around aimlessly in my kitchen, starving, and staring at a pantry and refrigerator full of foods that I could no longer enjoy. I remember feeling a lot of panic and anxiety… and hunger!

Family get-togethers and outings with friends became awkward. I would make a habit of eating before I left, and felt guilty at having to explain my restrictions to people around me who probably thought that I was just being fussy. Moving out on my own simplified the challenge – because when there's nothing in your home that you're not supposed to eat, you really can't slip in a moment of hunger. As you can imagine (and probably relate to), my new diet also turned into a very isolating experience.

Some relief came my way when I discovered prepared gluten-free foods in my regular supermarket. Gluten-free pastas, muffins, pizza crusts, breads, cake mixes, waffles and more made their way into my home. But despite their convenience, I could tell that this wasn't something I could sustain in my life. On top of being extremely expensive ($6 for a tiny loaf of frozen bread compared to my previous $0.99 fresh crusty breads) – it was hard to find anything that truly met all my needs. Something could be gluten-free, but still have dairy. Another wouldn't have dairy, but had yeast. And almost everything was packed full of sugar, potato or corn. Even with the marvels of the Internet, it was sometimes impossible, and almost always time consuming to find an elusive recipe that catered to every one of my dietary restrictions.

So I started looking up the ingredients on gluten-free pre-packaged foods in an attempt to "reverse engineer" my own recipes. There were so many new things I had never cooked with before – xanthan gum, carrageen, quinoa, tapioca flour, potato starch, arrowroot and more. Nearly all of my early experiments were minor disasters. Breads that turned out hard as rocks, bitter cookies, crumbling cakes… not to mention potato cookies.

Eventually, though, I learned *why* different ingredients are used and how to use them successfully. I learned about binding aids (to make foods stay together and not crumble to pieces), leavening aids (to make foods rise), fat content, moisture content, texture and flavour. With this new understanding, I finally figured out how to successfully substitute forbidden ingredients with acceptable ones.

Knowing how to substitute ingredients successfully is like knowing that 2+2 and 3+1 will both give you the same answer. If I can make a cake with wheat, all I have to do is make a few simple substitutions, and I'll end up with essentially the same end result. This knowledge has been my most powerful tool in adhering to my dietary needs in an affordable, satisfying and sustainable way. What started out as "there's nothing left for me to eat!" soon turned into "I can't believe how much food I never knew about!" Since changing my diet, I've enjoyed many new foods and new flavours that I probably would never have ventured to try otherwise. I've become extremely comfortable in the kitchen, I've learned where I can save heaps of money on food, and most importantly, I've improved my overall health immensely.

KNOWLEDGE IS POWER

What strikes me most in talking to others and in reading forum posts online, are the all-too-common stories of horror and failure. Some people have never had birthday cakes after being diagnosed with Celiac disease. Others constantly struggle to find gluten-free equivalents to their favourite foods, and many feel inadequate and embarrassed about their diet. A few people I know personally have even tried to eliminate gluten from their children's diets to deal with learning difficulties or autism, only to give up a few months later.

The saddest thing about these stories is that gluten-free, diary-free and sugar-free foods can taste great, don't have to be expensive, and can be easy to make! Reading these stories and watching people around me fumble and get discouraged ultimately motivated me into selling gluten-free cakes to try to help fill a void in peoples' lives. But even though I was helping people celebrate birthdays, baptisms and anniversaries – I wasn't helping anyone reach the point that I had reached. What were my customers doing the other 364 days in the year?

I have been fortunate to reach a point where eating without gluten, dairy and sugar has simply become my new normal way of life. This is the point that I want to help you reach. The point where cooking is easy. The point where you can make economical meals and special treats for you and your family. The point where you feel as comfortable with your new eating habits as you did with your old. The point where you feel liberated, empowered and inspired to make this change. This book won't be a miracle solution on its own; the biggest key to your success lies in your commitment and willpower to adhere to your diet. My experience has been a long journey, but I hope that this book makes yours just a little bit easier... and a whole lot shorter.

CHAPTER 2:
INSIDE THE KITCHEN

FOOD SAFETY

In this first section, we'll explore a few different aspects of food safety including how to minimize your exposure to food allergens and how to reduce your risk of food poisoning.

Cross Contamination

We all know how careful companies have to be when labelling foods that "may contain traces of nuts" because some people with these allergies can easily die from even the slightest exposure to nuts. Unfortunately, when it comes to less severe food allergens, manufacturers don't always show the same diligence. Ingredient labels won't always tell you about the risk of cross-contamination with wheat, dairy, soy, sugar, corn, or other common allergens.

Cross-contamination happens when safe to eat foods come into contact with unsafe or untolerated foods. This can happen in obvious ways, like placing cooked meats on the same dish as raw meats. But it can also happen in much less obvious ways, especially when it comes to processed food. In a factory that makes both regular and gluten-free cookies, for example, the gluten-free cookies it produces could be contaminated with gluten from any number of sources. Some examples of contamination can include wheat flour dust floating in the air and settling on gluten-free products or equipment; bits of cookie dough or flour stuck to machinery that is reused without proper cleaning; or even workers handling gluten and gluten-free products interchangeably. Unless the factory and its equipment are thoroughly cleaned between production batches, the gluten-free cookies could easily contain trace amounts of the allergen.

The lesson here is that even if something does not have gluten-containing ingredients listed on its label, it may still contain trace amounts which can be enough to make you sick and/or undermine your body's ability to heal. This goes for any other food allergen like dairy, corn, soy, sulphites, potato and more.

According to Health Canada, the only known way to reverse intestinal damage caused by Celiac disease is to strictly avoid all consumption of gluten. The following guidelines are meant to help you identify and minimize your risk of eating contaminated food. Celiacs and food allergy/intolerance sufferers should understand these carefully, as any exposure to even trace amounts of offending foods may cause a reaction and undermine your body's ability to heal and remain healthy. Know your own body, and get to know what you are able and unable to tolerate.

For simplicity – the guidelines below refer to gluten, but can be applied to any food allergen alike.

- Keep a separate designated area for preparing gluten-free foods – a section of the counter for example, and a cupboard. If you have to share counter space, always clean overhead, wall, and counter surfaces thoroughly for flour dust and crumbs.

- Always clean pots, pans and other shared items thoroughly (especially corners and edges) if they are also being used to cook gluten foods.

- Keep a separate set of cooking utensils to be used strictly for gluten-free foods. Store them in your own drawer or spoon holder.

- Opt for stainless steel or silicone if possible – if these utensils are ever contaminated, they will be much easier to clean than their porous wooden counterparts.

- Keep your own wooden cutting board and store it separately.

- Keep your own toaster oven and butter dish. If you have to share a toaster oven, choose one with a removable rack that you can wash thoroughly between uses.

- House members should always wash their hands after handling gluten foods and before touching common surfaces like refrigerator doors or oven handles.

- Prepare and put away gluten-free foods first.

My life has been much easier and less worrisome ever since I made my entire home gluten-free. This eliminates my worries around cross-contamination, and I no longer have to worry about the preparation guidelines above. The choice is ultimately yours. You can save time and make your life simpler by keeping a 100% gluten-free home, or save money by buying less expensive gluten products for the rest of your family.

Buyer Beware

When it comes to making smart shopping choices, here are few other helpful tips:

- Read your labels carefully and read them each time! Formulas can change and previously safe products may no longer be.
- Beware especially of ground foods like flours and pastas, as these carry a higher risk of cross-contamination than whole foods, especially if they have been processed on non-dedicated machinery.
- If in doubt, call the manufacturer and ask if the product in question was made in a dedicated gluten-free facility, or if it may contain traces of other allergens you are avoiding.
- Do not consume products if the manufacturer is evasive in their answers.
- Check your beauty products too! Dermal contact with gluten can sometimes cause reactions.
- Avoid bulk stores. Airborne particles from gluten flours may enter lungs and cause a reaction. Bins may also be contaminated from "double dipped" scoops.
- Deli meats often contain gluten. So, even if you choose gluten-free meat at a deli counter, it can get contaminated on deli slicing equipment or with improper handling.
- French fries can be contaminated if cooked in oil that was previously used to fry battered foods.
- Research restaurants before going out. If you're invited somewhere you're not familiar with, call and inquire ahead of time, or snack and stash before you go.
- Be prepared! Keep a small stash of safe snacks in your car, your purse, your office and in your home, so that you're never caught without anything to eat.

Basic Food Safety

Apart from avoiding food allergens, any cook should be aware of basic food safety principles. All meats and dairy products can very easily harbour pathogenic (harmful) bacteria and make you sick. So it's important to understand how to handle these foods properly and reduce the risk of infection.

Under optimal conditions, bacteria will divide and multiply every 20 minutes. Some bacteria can also enter a "spore" state where they will not grow, but will remain alive. There are six factors that affect bacterial growth: protein, temperature, water, pH, oxygen and time.

Bacteria thrives in the "danger zone" temperature range of 4-60°C (40-140°F). Meats and dairy products should never be left in this danger zone for more than two hours. Instead, keep food cooled below 4°C (40°F) and or heated just above 60°C (140°F). While this alone won't kill harmful bacteria, it will stop them from multiplying enough to make you sick. In order to kill most bacteria, food needs to be cooked to temperatures above 74°C (165°F). Use thermometers to check the internal temperature of your meats while they cook, and be aware of how long food is sitting out. Relying on your sense of smell or taste really isn't good enough because harmful bacteria can be odourless and tasteless.

Reducing the available water in meats through smoking, drying, adding sugar or adding salt can also slow bacterial growth, as can increasing food's acidity or alkalinity (pH). When it comes to oxygen, though, some bacteria grow in the presence of oxygen, while others grow in its absence. You can reduce your risk of food poisoning by controlling any one of the six factors discussed above, but the easiest thing to do is to keep hot foods hot and cold foods cold.

A few other rules of thumb for safe food handling:
- Refrigerate or freeze meats promptly when returning from the store. Keep an insulated bag or cooler in your trunk to keep food cool in transit.
- Use a meat thermometer to check the internal temperature of meats when cooking. Always insert the thermometer in the thickest section of meat (in the thigh or the centre of a roast, for example).

- Cook meats thoroughly until they have met the minimum temperatures below:

Food type	Cooking temperature °C (°F)
Whole poultry	82 (180)
Poultry parts, ground poultry or eggs	74 (165)
Pork, ground pork	71 (160)
Fish	70 (150)
Leftovers or casseroles	74 (165)

- Poultry should never be partially cooked, stored, and re-cooked later.
- Reheat foods quickly to at least their original cooking temperature.
- Never re-freeze thawed meats.
- Cool foods quickly in shallow dishes or in ice baths.
- Freeze foods below -18°C (-1°F).
- Always defrost meats in either cold running water or in the fridge. You can also defrost foods with your microwave.
- Never defrost meats on the counter or in an empty sink.
- Store raw meats on a drip proof tray on your refrigerator's bottom shelf or drawer away from cooked meats, vegetables and fruits.
- Never use the same utensils, dishes or cutting boards that have touched raw meats to handle cooked foods.
- Keep counters and sinks clean – don't leave standing water in your sink for long periods of time.
- Wash your hands thoroughly and often.
- If in doubt, throw it out.

Fire Safety

A Fire Chief once told me that one of the leading causes of house fires is unsafe cooking. So while we're on the subject food safety, here are a few tips on fire safety:

- Keep a fire extinguisher handy in your kitchen and maintain it according to the manufacturer's instructions.
- Always have a working smoke detector near your kitchen.
- Test your smoke detector monthly and change the batteries annually. Replace your smoke detector every 10 years.
- Keep your oven clean (try lining the bottom of the oven with aluminium foil to make cleanup easy and fast – check your owner's manual as this is not appropriate for all appliances).
- Keep heating surfaces clean to reduce smoke.
- Turn pot handles inwards towards the stove so that you don't accidentally topple over hot pots as you walk by.
- Never pour water on a grease fire. Use baking soda or a fire extinguisher suitable for grease fires, or smother with a lid.
- Never leave your stove unattended.
- Use timers to remind you to check your food.
- Your sense of smell is less effective when you are lying down – so don't be tempted to lie down or sleep while your food is cooking!

TOOLS OF THE TRADE

Now that you know how to be safe in your kitchen, let's move on to what you'll need to buy. This includes basic ingredients you should always keep on hand, as well as tools and equipment that can get you on your way.

Keeping Your Inventory – Filling Your Pantry

Most people keep a ready supply of staple items in their pantry because they use them often. Flour, sugar, spices, milk and eggs are just a few. To be successful with your new diet and save time and money, get in the habit of stocking the following gluten-free staples at all times:

- Brown rice flour, white rice flour or millet flour (or your favourite gluten-free flour)
- Tapioca flour
- Sweet rice flour (sometimes called glutinous rice flour)
- Baking soda and baking powder
- Unpasteurized honey
- Stevia (see Chapter 3 for buying tips)
- Eggs
- Soy milk, almond milk, rice milk, or other milk substitute
- Grapeseed oil (or other mild flavoured oil suitable for baking/frying)
- Extra virgin olive oil
- Sea salt and pepper
- Your favourite dried spices (e.g. garlic powder, oregano, basil, bay leaves, coriander, parley, thyme, cayenne, curry, cumin, cinnamon, nutmeg)

Flours can turn bitter if left out for a long period of time. So buy your flours either in quantities that you know you can use within 2-3 months, or keep extra flour in your freezer in a sealed bag. I buy my flours from Kinnikinnick (www.kinnikinnick.com) which is a company based in Edmonton, AB. They are a dedicated gluten-free, dairy-free and nut-free facility that ships flours out in conveniently sized 1kg vacuum sealed bags. I keep one bag out in my kitchen pantry for convenience, and store the rest in my freezer for freshness.

Equipment

If your budget is tight, you can get away with just a basic set of spoons, spatulas and dishes. I did this for several years before I started investing in small appliances. The amount of equipment you can get is almost endless, so I have split the lists below into "essential" and "optional" groups.

I highly recommend investing in high quality items that will last you a long time and that don't pose known or suspected risks to your health. Fortunately, some things like ceramic mixing bowls and glass measuring cups can be found commonly at garage sales, and can be easily disinfected. Other items like pots and pans, though, might be best purchased new.

When it comes to cookware and bakeware, you should always be conscious of the materials you are buying. According to the Alzheimer's Society of Canada, there is no conclusive evidence to link aluminium exposure to the development of Alzheimer's disease, but some researchers are still examining the link. If you're like me and simply wish to avoid aluminium cookware, stainless steel and cast iron are great alternatives. According to a 2007 study in Brazil, cooking food in cast iron pans can increase the iron content of the food. There are upper recommended limits for iron intake, so if you're going to cook with cast iron, be sure to discuss your iron levels with your doctor.

Perfluorinated chemicals (PFCs) have been associated with a number of adverse health effects in laboratory studies, according to Health Canada. In fact, the Canadian federal government has added some forms of PFC's to its Toxic Substances List under Schedule 1 of the *Canadian Environmental Protection Act, 1999*. Other forms of PFCs are currently being studied for possible future inclusion. These man-made chemicals are found widely in our environment, and are used in some non-stick coatings, scratch and stain resistant coatings and microwave popcorn bags. Outside the kitchen, they can also be found in stain resistant carpets, fabric and some cleaning products.

Bisphenol-A (BPA) is a chemical that has had a lot of recent attention. According to Health Canada, BPA is a suspected endocrine disrupter. It is commonly found in type 3 and type 7 polycarbonate plastic water bottles and containers, as well as in the linings of canned foods and drinks. Outside the kitchen, it is also found in electronic devices, CDs, sports equipment, dental fillings and medical devices. You can reduce your exposure to this chemical by using glass or unlined stainless steel water bottles and food storage containers (and yes, there are shatter-proof glass baby bottles available too). You should also avoid heating food or placing hot food in plastic.

When shopping for cookware or bakeware, look for glass, ceramic, uncoated stainless steel, or stone. Beware of cheap glass or ceramic from unknown origins as they may contain lead. Stainless steel may also cause reactions in individuals with sensitivities to nickel, but is generally considered safe to use. Some stainless steel cookware contains encapsulated aluminium and/or copper to help it heat more quickly and evenly. As long as they are fully encapsulated, these metals should not come in direct contact with your food.

Essential Tools
- At least 1 saucepan and 1 frying pan
- Rice cooker, non-coated stainless steel, preferably with an additional steaming basket
- Colander to rinse and drain fruits and veggies
- Small, fine sifter for sifting flours
- Good quality butcher's knife and small pairing knife
- Knife sharpener
- Wood cutting board, to be used only for gluten-free foods
- High quality vegetable peeler (for safety, invest in a good one)
- Cheese grater
- Cookie sheet, non-coated stainless steel
- Casserole dish, oven-safe
- Food storage containers, preferably glass or ceramic with sealing lids
- Mixing bowls (small, medium and large) in ceramic, glass, or stainless steel
- Set of measuring cups and measuring spoons
- 2 pot stirring spoons, wood or silicone
- 1 hard spatula and 1 flexible spatula
- Slotted spoon

Optional Tools
- High quality on-tap water filtration system
- Toaster oven, to reheat small amounts of food or cook small meals
- Manual egg whisk
- Garlic press
- Salad spinner
- Electric beater
- Food processor
- Blender
- Stand mixer

- Waffle iron
- Spice grinder (or mortar and pestle)
- Cake pan(s) up to 8" in diametre
- Small loaf pan
- Muffin tray
- Cookie cutters
- Icing tips and piping bag, icing spreader
- Lazy-Susan
- Vacuum sealer
- Upright freezer

Again, let me emphasize the importance of investing in good quality items for your kitchen. Good quality, well maintained knives are much safer to use than dull, unbalanced knives. And good quality items will generally last you much longer and save you time and money in the long run. Some things may be hard to find – like un-coated stainless steel rice cookers. I had to purchase mine online for more than double the cost of a cheap non-stick version in stores. So far though, it has worked wonderfully, the interior doesn't scratch and I know I'm not eating PFC's with my rice.

BEING EFFICIENT WITH YOUR TIME

Cooking can be fun and rewarding – but let's face it – most of us don't have the luxury (or motivation) to be cooking elaborate meals day after day. Convenience and time will often lure us towards take out, fast food or prepared frozen meals. So why not make the convenience yourself? Learning how to buy, prepare and store in bulk can help you stick to your diet by saving you time and money.

Buying in Bulk

One of my most useful strategies for saving time has been to buy, cook and store in bulk. Buying in bulk can come in many forms. Personally, I prefer to buy meats in larger quantities from respectable local farms. When I visit my local farmer's market, I first speak with the farmers to understand how they feed and treat their animals. For healthier and ethically raised meats, look for grass-fed animals that actually go outside and live normal lives. ("Access to outdoors" is a term that is often used to describe free-range chickens, but this term can be misleading and doesn't necessarily mean that the animals have actually ever gone outside.) When I do buy, I will often purchase large enough quantities to last me 3-4 months. This drastically cuts down on my shopping trips, and I really only end up buying fresh fruits and veggies once a week or less. If you're lucky, you may even be able to find farmers who will deliver straight to your own home.

Storing in Bulk

A few years ago, I bought a vacuum sealer to separate and store meats because I was getting tired of freezer burn. A vacuum sealer is also handy to split and store your own meals and cooked foods into single servings. This saves an enormous amount of time, because it takes much less time to cook and store one big batch of food than it does to cook the same dish over and over again. It's also a healthy and convenient alternative to processed and packaged TV dinners. You can store everything from steamed rice to vegetables, chillies, beans, lentils, cooked/sliced sausages and more. By storing cooked foods in single serving sizes, your freezer can become your very own ready-to-eat aisle, and you'll be able to throw a meal together in minutes.

The trick to storing food is to pack items as *flat* as possible to make it easier and faster to reheat. You should also make sure there is as little air as possible in contact with your food so that you don't end up with freezer burn – not to mention money in the garbage. Vacuum sealers are great, but if you don't have one, or are only planning to freeze food for a short period of time, you can simply squeeze as much air as possible out of resealable bags. To reheat, simply place your frozen food into a saucepan with a small amount of oil and water, then cover and steam over medium-low heat for 5-10 minutes until hot throughout.

A few years ago, my husband and I invested in an upright freezer so that we could store more food and make fewer trips to the store. My freezer also makes it easy for me to store home-made packaged meals and stock up on things like frozen blueberries when they're on sale. We chose an upright freezer because it's much easier to organize and see everything in an upright appliance than in a chest model. This is a big plus when it comes to reducing "forgotten" food going to waste. A disadvantage to an upright model, however, is that an open door will let cold air escape faster (so decide what you want before you open the door). It can also be more expensive to purchase. If you do decide to buy a freezer, be sure to set it to -18°C (-1°F) or lower to keep food safe.

Cooking Meals For a Family With a Variety of Needs

If you're trying to accommodate various dietary needs and preferences, my best advice is to keep it simple. I've seen too many people try to cook three separate meals <u>per</u> meal... everyday! One meal for a vegetarian daughter, another for a son with learning difficulties trying a gluten-free diet, and another "normal" meal for a sceptical meat loving spouse. I can't even imagine how much work that would be! Add to that the constant attention to cross-contamination if one member is Celiac, and you have failure lurking around the corner.

Instead of looking at meals as single dish masterpieces, cook your meals as mix and match delights. Throw some brown rice in your rice cooker when you get home, or about 40 minutes before you plan to serve dinner. Cook one or two simple vegetable dishes and a meat dish separately. Then serve everything separately, sit down and enjoy. Everyone can pick and choose what they want and can eat. If you're accommodating a vegetarian, be sure to have a protein rich dish available. Try substituting quinoa for rice; adding tofu to veggie dishes; or including lentils, beans, eggs, fish or cheese.

And who says that everyone can't enjoy the same dish? I have many times entertained friends with a pasta dish or a lasagne made with brown rice pasta and goat cheese to everyone's delight (and to their surprise – "this isn't wheat!?").

SUMMARY

- Be aware of and avoid potential cross-contamination risks.
- Practice safe food handling techniques.
- Start building your inventory of kitchen tools and appliances with essential items, and invest in good quality equipment.
- Save time by buying, storing and cooking in bulk.
- Keep meals simple to more easily accommodate various dietary needs.

CHAPTER 3:
MAKING SUCCESSFUL SUBSTITUTIONS

SUBSTITUTIONS

The majority of this chapter focuses on how to make successful substitutions so that you can take almost any recipe you find and adapt it to your specific needs. Substituting for meats, veggies, grains, and their complimentary spices is pretty straight forward. Later in this chapter, you will find some helpful lists, descriptions and charts for substituting common meats, veggies and grains. These will be helpful if you need to avoid something in particular, or if you are simply missing a few ingredients for a recipe.

Where things can get tricky is in baking. Before you can successfully substitute for any ingredient, you will first have to understand what it *does*. Once you understand how it contributes to the end texture, flavour, nutritional value and overall character of a dish – you'll be able to replace it successfully and almost unnoticeably. For this reason, each section below on wheat/gluten, dairy, refined sugar, soy and corn, will explore the following:

- The basic characteristics of the food discussed
- Where it is commonly found
- Hidden sources
- Alternative foods, their characteristics and when best to use them
- Substitution equivalents

Finally, at the end of this chapter, we'll discuss the basic rules of thumb for substitutions in baking and how to troubleshoot and improve your recipes.

GLUTEN AND WHEAT

Wheat is a cultivated grass that originated in Western Asia. It is most often milled into flour to make breads, cookies, cakes, cereal, pasta, noodles and couscous. Wheat can also be fermented to make beer, alcohol, vodka and biofuel. Gluten is a nutritional protein that is found in wheat, and also in barley, rye, kamut, spelt and their derivatives.

When mixed with water, the gluten protein develops to create an elastic dough that can hold gas. Gluten's distinctive elastic and sticky quality explains why gluten-*free* foods tend to be more crumbly and dense. This stickiness is the reason that wheat pastries become tough and less flaky when you over-handle their dough. It's also the reason that wheat based breads and cakes can rise much easier and yield fluffy delights like angel food cake. Finally, gluten helps foods retain moisture, which is why gluten-free baked goods are best stored in sealed containers at room temperature when possible because they will dry out very easily.

Wheat and gluten are some of the most difficult foods to eliminate from our diets. They are extremely common in North American foods, popping up in everything from soups to liquorice to pastas and breads. To successfully avoid wheat/gluten, you have to be informed and vigilant at all times. It's surprising how many times I've been out, have said that I don't eat wheat, and still been offered bread, pasta and cakes. (Question, "Do you have gluten-free pasta?" Reply, "No, but we have whole-wheat pasta!")

There are a number of reasons that people must or choose to avoid wheat and gluten. Celiac disease is an autoimmune disorder where the body mistakenly attacks its own intestinal lining in reaction to being exposed to gluten. This can cause serious damage and complications because intestinal damage reduces a person's ability to absorb a number of nutrients, vitamins, protein and fat. According to Health Canada's publication, *Celiac Disease – The Gluten Connection*, symptoms of Celiac disease can include diarrhea, anaemia, nutritional deficiencies, bone or joint pain, indigestion, nausea, constipation, mouth ulcers, infertility, miscarriages, depression, migraines, fatigue, weight loss (although some Celiacs can be overweight) and unexplained neurological conditions. Celiac disease can be tricky to detect because symptoms can vary widely in type and severity and are often ignored for years or even decades before being properly investigated.

Thankfully, though, Celiac disease can be effectively treated by strictly avoiding gluten.

Even if you don't have Celiac disease, gluten can adversely affect your health if you are allergic or intolerant to it. Just as with other allergic reactions, gluten allergy symptoms can include runny nose, watery eyes, excess mucous, inflammation and skin irritations, brought on by the body's production of histamines. Intolerance or sensitivity to gluten, on the other hand, does not involve the immune system, but is rather caused by the body's inability to properly digest or absorb the offending food. Gluten or wheat intolerance can also be difficult to diagnose and can contribute to a wide range of symptoms. Some research has even shown that autistic children can benefit from gluten-free and casein-free diets.

Commonly found in:
- Wheat (triticum), barley (hordeum), rye (secale)
- Kamut, spelt
- Pastas, pastries, breads, cereals
- Alcohol (beer and some spirits)

Look out for:
- Blue cheese (when made with wheat flour or bread)
- Brewers yeast
- Bulgur
- Coffee substitutes
- Couscous
- Graham flour
- Hydrolyzed wheat protein
- Imitation bacon
- Malt (usually derived from barley)
- Modified starch, modified food starch
- Monosodium glutamate (MSG)
- Oats (avena), which can often be contaminated with gluten
- Processed meats
- Semolina
- Thickened soups, broths or gravies

- Titricale
- Vegetable starch
- Wheat bran/flour/germ/starch/gluten

Hidden sources:
- Cereals sweetened with barley malt extract
- Certain food colourings, additives and flavourings
- Flavoured drinks, including chocolate milk
- Flavoured nuts, chips
- Flour or cake mixes (always read the ingredient label)
- Liquorice and candies
- Malt vinegars
- Processed and pre-packaged foods
- Processed meats
- Salad dressings
- Some medications and vitamins
- Soya sauce

Characteristics:
- Product bulk and volume
- Binding aid (sticky)
- Leavening aid (helps baked goods rise)

Safe Store Bought Foods:
- Gluten-free breads, muffins, buns or cold cereals
- Gluten-free hot cereal grains: cream of buckwheat, cream of rice
- Gluten-free grains: millet, quinoa, buckwheat, rice
- Gluten-free pasta (choose brown rice pasta for higher fibre)

Substituting For Wheat And Gluten

When substituting for regular flour in a recipe, it's important to remember that gluten is both a binding (sticky) and a leavening (rising) aid. What this means is if you were to simply use one cup of brown rice flour in place of wheat flour, for example, you would end up with a very flat, dense and crumbly product. So, while you can use a gluten-free flour to substitute for the "bulk" of wheat flour, you have to look to other ingredients to make up for its binding and leavening qualities.

Wheat Flour as Bulk

Wheat flour normally makes the "bulk" of baked goods; that is it makes up most of their volume and mass. In my kitchen, I most often use brown rice flour as the bulk substitute for wheat flour. I prefer to use brown rice over white rice flour for its superior nutritional value and its richer texture. I also find that brown rice flour has a mild taste, nice texture, is easy to find and is relatively inexpensive. Some people may develop sensitivities to rice because the grain is related to wheat. If this happens to you, choose something else and try not to eat rice more often than once every four days. Here is a list of several flours that you can use to substitute for bulk:

Brown rice flour – slightly nutty flavour, medium texture, easy to find
White rice flour – milder in flavour, finer texture but lower in fibre
Millet flour – nuttier, slightly grittier, good substitute for corn meal
Quinoa flour – high in protein, can be expensive
Amaranth flour – nutty flavour, can be expensive and is harder to find
Teff flour – strong flavoured dark flour, can be expensive
Coconut flour – unique flavour, more moist

Gluten as a Binding (Sticky) Aid

Gluten as a binding aid keeps baked goods together and prevents them from crumbling apart. Depending on what you want to achieve, the best substitutes for gluten's binding qualities are starches and gelatines. Below is a substitution chart that you can use as a quick reference guide. Remember that when you are trying to substitute for 1 cup of wheat flour, whatever combination of ingredients you choose should add up to approximately the same amount.

Binding aid	Best for	Substitution for 1 cup wheat flour
Tapioca starch (also labelled as tapioca flour)	Dense baked goods such as pizza crusts and crackers. Great for thickening sauces and gravies. Can also work well in cakes. Very similar to arrowroot flour, but much cheaper.	3/4 cup brown rice flour 1/4 cup tapioca starch 1/2 tsp baking powder
Arrowroot flour	Dense baked goods such as pizza crusts and crackers. Can also work well in cakes. Can be expensive.	3/4 cup brown rice flour 1/4 cup arrowroot flour 1/2 tsp baking powder
Arrowroot powder	Most baked goods. Can be expensive.	1 cup brown rice flour 1 tbsp arrowroot powder 1/2 tsp baking powder
Sweet rice flour	Delicate baked goods such as cakes, cupcakes, waffles. Yields very moist and light products.	1/2 cup brown rice flour 1/2 cup sweet rice flour 1/2 tsp baking powder
Gelatine (animal based) OR Agar flakes (algae based / vegan)	Great for thickening desserts such as custards, jams or pie fillings. I prefer not to use this for gravies as it tends to make them gelatinous instead of creamy and thick.	1 tsp of gelatine or agar flakes dissolved in warm water will generally thicken approximately 1 cup of liquid ingredients

You can find the metric version of this table on page 164

In my own personal kitchen, I keep a ready supply of brown rice flour, tapioca starch and sweet rice flour. Having these three ingredients on hand at all times allows me to make almost any recipe that calls for wheat flour, and they are all relatively inexpensive to buy.

Tapioca starch comes from the cassava plant which is a root vegetable. It will yield essentially the same results as arrowroot flour for a fraction of the price. You can buy inexpensive tapioca starch in small packages at Chinese grocery stores, and at some bulk grocers. If you are Celiac or require strict avoidance, however, you should buy from manufacturers with dedicated gluten-free facilities, and should not shop in bulk stores. Kinnikinnick (www.kinnikinnick.com based in Canada) and Bob's Red Mill (www.bobsredmill.com based in the U.S.) are good places to start.

To thicken soups, sauces and stews, simply dissolve 1 tbsp tapioca starch in a small amount of cold water, and stir it into the soup or sauce as it is simmering. Add more to achieve your desired thickness. Too much tapioca starch will make foods very chewy and can make liquids gummy or lumpy.

Arrowroot starch or flour is a root starch from the arrowroot plant. Just as with tapioca starch, arrowroot can be dissolved and used to thicken liquids. Once your soup or sauce has thickened, however, it should be removed from the heat, as arrowroot will break down when overcooked.

Sweet rice flour is sometimes called "glutinous rice flour" for its sticky texture – but it does not actually contain nutritional gluten. I use sweet rice flour for my delicate baked goods to produce surprisingly moist and light cakes.

Gelatine and Agar both have binding qualities that harden clear, and do not create cloudiness. These are ideal choices for desserts and jellies.

Many pre-packaged gluten-free foods use corn or potato starch as a binding aid. I have even seen cookies that were just made of corn starch, sugar and baking powder (yuck!). Unfortunately, corn and potato are two other common allergens, so I have not included them in the previous chart. We'll cover corn in a later section.

I also have not included other options such as xanthan gum, carrageen, chick pea (garbanzo) flour or psyllium because I like to keep things simple in my kitchen and don't like to keep a vast inventory of different ingredients. If you come across these ingredients in a recipe but don't have them, simply look at the total amount of flours and binders called for, and substitute the total volume with the ingredients that you have available in your own kitchen. I will illustrate this process in an example later in this chapter.

Gluten as a Leavening (Rising) Aid

So far, we've covered the bulk and binding aspects of gluten. As you'll remember, gluten is also a leavening aid, which means it helps baked goods rise because it can hold gas. If you're like me and have tried every kind of gluten-free bread in the store, you'll know that gluten-free breads are never as light and fluffy as wheat bread – this is why. Unfortunately, gluten-free baked goods will never be as fluffy as wheat goods, but with a few slight changes we can still come very, very close. Typical leavening ingredients include yeast, baking soda and baking powder. Eggs (which also have binding qualities) and soy lecithin are also useful for this purpose.

Yeast is a living single cell fungal organism. When fed with sugar in a warm and humid environment, yeast will multiply and release gas as it grows. This gas is what makes dough rise. Remember, one of gluten's characteristics is that it is elastic and able to hold gas. Because of this, gluten-free yeast dough often requires double the yeast of regular wheat recipes. I caution you on baking too many yeast recipes, especially if you are detoxifying. According to a study conducted by researchers at the University of Minnesota in 2002, yeast that is not kept in check by friendly bacteria and a healthy immune response in the intestine, can transform from its single cell form to a fungal form. In its fungal form, yeast can penetrate the intestinal wall and thus contribute to the development of leaky-gut syndrome. If you have other existing digestive issues or have recently taken antibiotics, you may also be more susceptible to yeast overgrowth. So instead of making yeast breads, try a quick bread (yeast-free) or sourdough bread.

Baking soda is a base (opposite of an acid). When it is mixed in with an acidic batter, the reaction creates gas. Just think about how much foam and gas is created when you mix vinegar with baking soda – this is essentially what happens in baked goods. Measure baking soda carefully in recipes. Adding too much baking soda will give your food a bitter aftertaste.

Baking powder is a combination of a base and an acid. When mixed with liquid ingredients, these two components blend and react to create gas. Since baking powder is both base and acid, it does not necessarily require an acidic batter to make it rise like baking soda does. Because of this balance, you can add more baking powder to recipes without changing its flavour. For large cakes, I often double the baking powder called for when modifying a gluten recipe. Smaller treats like muffins should be topped up more moderately. Too much baking powder will make cakes rise quickly in the oven, but fall and collapse once removed.

Commercial baking powder is usually made of baking soda, cream of tartar and corn starch (some brands use wheat starch and therefore contain gluten). If you are avoiding corn or are unsure if your baking powder is gluten-free, you can make your own by mixing 1 part baking soda, 2 parts cream of tartar and 1 part tapioca starch.

Eggs are a wonderful ingredient for baked goods. They act as a leavening aid, a binding aid, and also add moisture because of their fat content. If your cake is too dry, dense or crumbly, try adding an extra egg, and omitting 1 cup of liquid ingredients (water or milk). Alternatively, add 1 egg and add 3/4 to 1 cup of additional bulk flour. Too many eggs will give cakes an "eggy" flavour and can adversely affect its texture. Don't be afraid to experiment – you can always try again!

Cook in smaller dishes. This is my final tip for making doughs and batters rise. The bigger your dish, the harder it is for a cake or bread to rise in the centre. If you bake a cake in too large a dish, it will not rise in the centre and you'll end up with a cake that's hard along the edges and raw in the middle. For best results, stick to 8 inch (20cm) pans or smaller.

Substitution Examples

Now that we know how to substitute for wheat and gluten, let's walk through a couple of examples. The following two recipe examples are for chocolate chip cookies. In the first example, we'll walk through transforming a regular recipe into a gluten-free recipe; and in the second example, we'll walk through making substitutions to an already gluten-free recipe.

Example 1a) Chocolate Chip Cookies (regular recipe)

3/4 cup	Sugar	2–1/4 cups	All-purpose flour
3/4 cup	Brown sugar	1 tsp	Baking soda
1 cup	Butter	3/4 tsp	Salt
2	Eggs	2 cups	Chocolate chips
1 tsp	Vanilla extract		

The first thing to do is to mark which ingredients you cannot tolerate. If you're just avoiding gluten, this would include the flour, and possibly the chocolate chips. From the earlier chart, we know 1 cup of flour = 3/4 cup brown rice flour + 1/4 cup of tapioca starch. Now, the math to convert 2–1/4 cups of flour might not be so easy to do in your head. Luckily, the substitution chart is just a guideline, not an exact science. So to make the numbers easy, let's simply substitute 2–1/4 cups flour for 1-3/4 cups brown rice flour and 1/2 cup of tapioca starch. We won't add additional leavening aids since cookies don't really need to rise much anyways. Our new recipe becomes:

Example 1b) Modified Chocolate Chip Cookies

3/4 cup	Sugar	*1–3/4 cups*	*Brown rice flour*
3/4 cup	Brown sugar	*1/2 cup*	*Tapioca starch*
1 cup	Butter	1 tsp	Baking soda
2	Eggs	3/4 tsp	Salt
1 tsp	Vanilla extract	2 cups	Chocolate chips

If you prefer a soft cookie over a crunchy cookie, use sweet rice flour instead of tapioca starch. The ratio for using sweet rice flour and brown rice flour as substitutes is around 50/50. In this case, our conversion goes from 2-1/4 cups of flour to 1-1/8 cups of brown rice flour, and 1-1/8 cups of sweet rice flour. Again, this isn't an exact science, so if it's easier to measure, you can simply use 1-1/4 cup of brown rice flour and 1 cup of sweet rice flour.

Example 1c) Modified Chocolate Chip Cookies (soft)

3/4 cup	Sugar	*1–1/4 cups*	*Brown rice flour*
3/4 cup	Brown sugar	*1 cup*	*Sweet rice flour*
1 cup	Butter	1 tsp	Baking soda
2	Eggs	3/4 tsp	Salt
1 tsp	Vanilla extract	2 cups	Chocolate chips

The key in this exercise is to maintain the same *total* volume of flour as in the original recipe. Don't be overwhelmed with exact conversions – as long as you're relatively close it should turn out fine.

Next, we'll look at an example of a recipe that is already gluten-free. The problem you might face in this case, is not necessarily having all the ingredients for this particular recipe in your kitchen pantry. Let's take a look:

Example 2a) Chocolate Chip Cookies (gluten-free)

2-1/4 cup	Quinoa flour	3/4 cup	Sugar
1/2 tsp	Xanthan gum	3/4 cup	Brown sugar
1 tsp	Baking soda	1 tsp	Vanilla
1/2 tsp	Salt	2	Eggs
1 tbsp	Milk	12 oz	Chocolate chips
4 oz	Butter		

First, let's look over the recipe, and figure out what was used as the bulk flour and as the binding aids. In this case, the bulk flour is quinoa and the binding aid is xanthan gum. If you need to use different ingredients, the same guidelines for substitutions will still apply.

Remember, our goal is to substitute for the *total volume* of flours. In this case, we need to substitute 2-1/4 cups (plus a half teaspoon of xanthan gum, but this is not significant). Sound familiar? All you have to do is replace the quinoa flour and xanthan gum with the same ratios of brown rice flour/tapioca starch or brown rice flour/sweet rice flour as we did previously in example 1. So in this case, our recipe becomes:

Example 2b) Modified Chocolate Chip Cookies (gluten-free)

1-3/4 cup	*Brown rice flour*	3/4 cup	Sugar
1/2 cup	*Tapioca starch*	3/4 cup	Brown sugar
1 tsp	Baking soda	1 tsp	Vanilla
1/2 tsp	Salt	2	Eggs
1 tbsp	Milk	12 oz	Chocolate chips
4 oz	Butter		

Dairy

Dairy intolerance symptoms, just like gluten and wheat intolerance symptoms, arise from the body's inability to properly digest or absorb the offending food. Individuals who are lactose intolerant do not produce enough lactase enzymes to fully break down lactose. According to the National Institute of Arthritis and Musculoskeletal and Skin Diseases, undigested lactose can cause indigestion, bloating, gas, nausea and diarrhea.

Undigested lactose also creates lactic acid in the intestine, which may explain why some studies have even shown that individuals with lactose intolerance are at greater risk for developing osteoporosis. Some people who are lactose intolerant may also be sensitive to the casein protein in animal milk. So if you are lactose intolerant and are taking lactase enzymes to drink milk, you may only be addressing part of the problem.

If you are allergic to milk, your body will produce histamines in reaction to dairy exposure. Dairy allergy symptoms can include skin irritations (eczema, rash), excessive mucous build-up (having to clear your throat), wheezing, asthma or rhinitis.

Whenever I tell people that I do not consume cow dairy, most will ask me how I get enough calcium. Personally, I find it strange that people feel it's so important to drink milk into adulthood in order to be healthy. If you think about it, humans are the only species that regularly drink another animal's milk, and are the only species that drink milk past infancy. As for maintaining a well-balanced diet that is rich in calcium and vitamin D, look no further than dark leafy greens, sunshine, and high quality nutritional supplements.

Commonly found in:
Milk
Yogurt
Butter
Cheese
Cream
Ice cream
Icings and frostings
Chocolate
Baked goods

Look out for:
Artificial butter flavour
Casein
Lactose
Milk protein or milk solids
Modified milk ingredients
Rennet
Whey

Hidden sources:
Artificial butter, butter fat/flavour/oil
Battered and deep fried foods
Brown sugar
Candy
Caramel colouring/flavouring
Casein in wax used to coat some fresh fruits
Creamy soups
Egg/fat substitutes
Flavoured coffee, coffee whitener, non-dairy creamers
Flavoured snack foods
High protein flour
Margarine
Natural flavouring
Prescription drugs and vitamins
Processed meats and foods

Characteristics
Creamy texture
Slightly sweet flavour

Substitutions

Milk is one of the hardest ingredients to avoid in pre-packaged foods, but is fortunately one of the easiest ingredients to substitute when cooking. What you decide to use as a substitute should be based purely on preference and need. Use the following charts to substitute for both milk and butter.

Ingredient	Best for	Substitution for 1 cup cow milk
Soy milk (look for unsweetened)	Any baked goods, cereal, coffee, drinks and smoothies	1 cup soy milk
Almond milk (look for unsweetened)	Any baked goods, cereal, coffee, drinks and smoothies	1 cup almond milk
Goat milk or sheep milk	Any savoury foods like pasta sauces	1 cup goat or sheep milk
Rice milk (I recommend brown rice milk)	Any baked goods, cereal, coffee, drinks and smoothies.	1 cup rice milk
Water	Anytime you open your cupboard and realize you've run out of milk substitutes!	1 cup water

Ingredient	Best for	Substitution for 1 cup butter
Grapeseed Oil	Use in place of butter in baked goods	3/4 cup grapeseed oil
Olive Oil	Use in place of butter in savoury dishes	3/4 cup olive oil

You can find the metric version of this table on page 165

Soy milk is a nice rich and creamy substitute. According to a Canadian study conducted in 2006, soy products contain high levels of isoflavones and phytoestrogens. Health Canada currently recognizes the use of soybean extracts and isolates in nutritional supplements for reducing bone mineral density loss and menopausal symptoms in women. While the estrogenic effects of soy might be beneficial to some women, they may not be so for men, so it is best enjoyed in moderation. Consult your doctor if you are unsure. (Soy is also another common food allergen and should be avoided by some.) There are many soy milk choices on the market, but some of the better brands that I have tried include So Good, So Nice, and Sunrise. Soy milk is also very easy to make. Look for unsweetened versions as many have added sugar.

Almond milk is also quite easy to find in regular grocery stores. It has a pleasantly smooth and creamy texture and is similarly priced to rice milk. It's great for baking and for pouring over cereals. Look for unsweetened versions as many have added sugar.

Rice milk comes in many different varieties. Some are quite unappetizing, but others are quite nice. My favourite rice milk brand is Ryza (www.ryza.ca). Ryza is made from brown rice and is naturally sweet, even though it doesn't contain any added sugar. This is a great milk substitute for baked goods, smoothies and cereals.

Goat milk is available in most grocery stores today and is the creamiest substitute I've tried. Some people that cannot tolerate cow milk can actually consume goat (or sheep) milk without any issues. It does have a unique taste that may need some getting used to. Generally, though, you can't really tell the difference when you use it in recipes. If you want to switch your kids from drinking cow to goat milk, try mixing small amounts of goat milk with cow milk at first, and gradually increase the proportion of goat milk until you've completely eliminated the cow milk. Be sure to check with your paediatrician if you plan to feed goat milk to your baby.

Water of course is our wonderful natural resource that many of us take for granted. Be friendly to the planet and its natural aquifers – choose tap water instead of bottled. Bottled water is not necessarily any more "pure" than tap water. For the past six years, I have used a high quality on-tap water filtration unit which removes traces of lead, petrochemicals, prescription drugs and other impurities. From an environmental perspective, a water filtration system doesn't require importing water, as some bottled water products do, and can also reduce the amount of waste you create.

Grapeseed oil is a mild tasting oil that will not affect the flavour of your baked goods. This oil makes an excellent substitute for butter. It also has a high smoking point, which makes it a good oil for frying or cooking at higher temperatures.

Olive oil is a very healthy source of fat, and great substitute for butter. Extra virgin olive oil has a distinctive flavour that works best with meats, veggies and other savoury dishes. This oil has a low smoking point, and should only be cooked at medium or low temperatures.

Substitution Example

Let's revisit our earlier chocolate chip cookie recipe, only this time we'll also substitute for dairy to make it both gluten-free and dairy-free.

Modified Chocolate Chip Cookies (Gluten-Free) from page 28

3/4 cup	Sugar	*1–3/4 cups*	*Brown rice flour*
3/4 cup	Brown sugar	*1/2 cup*	*Tapioca starch*
1 cup	Butter	1 tsp	Baking soda
2	Eggs	3/4 tsp	Salt
1 tsp	Vanilla extract	2 cups	Chocolate chips

There are two dairy ingredients in this recipe: butter and chocolate chips. Let's start by substituting the butter with 3/4 cup grapeseed oil. Now, since this means we're substituting a dry/hard ingredient (butter) with a wet one (oil), our batter is going to become runny from the additional liquid content. Whenever you need to make this type of dry-to-wet substitution, it's a good idea to add back dry ingredients equal to about half the volume of the additional liquid. In this example, let's compensate for the extra 3/4 cup of liquid content by adding an extra 1/2 cup of flours to the recipe (we'll split this into 1/4 cup brown rice flour and 1/4 cup tapioca starch).

For chocolate chips, we have a few options to choose from. If you can find them, choose dairy-free chocolate chips or carob chips. If neither is available to you, use raisins, dried fruit or nuts instead. Our recipe now becomes this:

Modified Chocolate Chip Cookies (Gluten-Free and Dairy-Free)

3/4 cup	Sugar	*2 cups*	*Brown rice flour*
3/4 cup	Brown sugar	*3/4 cup*	*Tapioca starch*
3/4 cup	*Grapeseed oil*	1 tsp	Baking soda
2	Eggs	3/4 tsp	Salt
1 tsp	Vanilla extract	*2 cups*	*Chocolate chips**

*Dairy-free

SUGAR

Sugars and carbohydrates come in many forms and can each behave differently in our bodies. The way that your body metabolizes sugars and carbohydrates can be measured by what's called a glycemic index. According to the Canadian Diabetes Association, foods with a low to medium glycemic index can help control your blood glucose level, thereby providing you with more constant and longer lasting energy. High glycemic index foods, on the other hand, will cause a greater spike in your blood glucose level, which can lead to an energy high and subsequent crash. Lower glycemic foods include whole grains, meats and many fruits and vegetables. Higher glycemic foods, on the other hand, include many refined foods like white sugar, white rice and processed food. But don't be fooled – high glycemic foods also include tropical fruits, carrots and even white potatoes.

In this section, I will focus only on identifying sources of and substituting for white table sugar, and not naturally occurring sugars. White sugar is generally derived from corn, sugar cane (related to wheat) and/or beets, which might be part of the problem for corn or wheat allergy sufferers. If you are experiencing problems with yeast, you may also benefit from eating less sugar, and increasing your in-take of lower glycemic index foods, since yeast needs sugar to grow.

Commonly found in:
Baked goods
Most pre-packaged foods and packaged drinks
Candies, snacks

Hidden sources:
Processed meats
Sauces
Soups

Look out for:
Ingredient names ending in "-ose" (glucose, fructose, dextrose, etc.)

Characteristics:
Sweetener
Adds moisture and texture to baked goods

Creates small air pockets when beaten with butter/fats to make frostings fluffy
Can be sticky (binding)
Necessary to make yeast grow when leavening dough (making it rise)
Used with some pectins to harden jellies and jams

Substitutions

Unless you're making a fluffy frosting, you should generally only worry about substituting for sugar's sweetness. If you're substituting white sugar for a liquid sweetener, you will have to compensate for the additional liquid content in your recipe. To do this, it's a good idea to either omit the same amount of liquid elsewhere in the recipe, or to add dry ingredients equal to about half the sweetener's volume (e.g. add 1/2 cup of flour for every 1 cup of liquid sweetener).

Ingredient	Best for	Substitution for 1 cup refined white sugar
Stevia*	Baked goods, drinks	1/4 tsp powdered OR 10 drops of liquid stevia
Honey	Baked goods, drinks, smoothies, spreads	3/4 cup unpasteurized honey
Maple syrup	Baked goods, pancakes/waffles	3/4 cup maple syrup
Agave nectar*	Baked goods, pancakes/waffles	3/4 cup agave nectar
Xylitol*	Baked goods, frostings	1 cup xylitol
Rice syrup	Baked goods, snack bars	1 cup rice syrup
Fruit juice	Baked goods, drinks, smoothies	1 cup fruit juice
Molasses (related to wheat)	Gingerbread cookies, baked goods calling for brown sugar	3/4 cup molasses

You can find the metric version of this table on page 166
*Safe for diabetics. Check with your doctor and test your blood glucose levels regularly.

Stevia is a leaf extract that comes from a shrub native to Paraguay. Most people that I've met who have tried stevia think that it has a bitter aftertaste. After trying a number of brands and variations myself, I have found that pure forms of stevia are actually very pleasant and do not have an aftertaste at all. Look for powdered stevia that lists only stevia in the ingredient list, or liquid stevia that lists only stevia and water. Stevia mixed with silica, glycerine or alcohol tends to have an aftertaste.

Unpasteurized honey contains beneficial enzymes and nutrients and can have many health benefits. My personal favourite is creamed, raw unpasteurized borage honey that I buy from a local beekeeper. Don't be shy to try out different kinds of honey as each will have its own distinctive flavour. Health Canada warns parents not to feed honey to infants under the age of one year, as they may contract botulism. Honey is not recommended during yeast cleanses.

Maple syrup is easily my favourite sweetener of all and imparts a lovely flavour to cakes. Maple syrup is available as number 1, 2 and 3 varieties, with n°1 being the lightest in colour and flavour, and n°3 being the darkest and having the strongest maple taste. I like to use a blend of stevia and n°2 maple syrup in my cakes to take advantage of each ingredient's benefits. Most grocery stores will only carry n°1 syrups, so check out your local farmer's market to get the other varieties directly from the source. Be careful not to use too much maple syrup in baked goods, though, as it can burn easily in the oven. Maple syrup is not recommended during yeast cleanses. Avoid imitation maple syrup which usually contains refined sugar and corn.

Agave nectar is a light syrup that resembles something of a cross between corn syrup and maple syrup. It's great for drizzling over pancakes, waffles, and desserts, and you can also use it to bake. Currently, agave is quite expensive, so I generally save this as a special treat.

Xylitol is a sugar that is derived either from birch trees or from corn and is substituted 1:1 for sugar. According to a 2003 study in California, xylitol promotes dental health and is not readily metabolized by microorganisms. Because of its similar granular structure to sugar, it's the best substitute for sugar in frostings. If you plan on trying to use xylitol, it is recommended that you "ease" your system into it as it can cause indigestion in those who have not consumed it before. Start with 1 tsp (5ml) per day and work your way up.

Rice syrup is gluten-free, unlike many other barley derived malts. It is very sticky and thick. It is quite similar to corn syrup – not too sweet, and mild in taste. I like to use rice malt to make nut bars or seed cookies that don't require much cooking.

Fruit juice is very easy to find and simple to use. Be sure to read labels carefully because many fruit juices contain added refined sugar. Fruit juice will add a lot of liquid to your recipes. Your best bet is to substitute any milk or water in your recipe with juice and simply omit the sugar – this way your batter won't turn out runny. Grape juice, apple juice, pineapple juice and pear juice are great choices and each will add a characteristic flavour to your recipes. To compliment a fruit juice sweetened cake, try adding the same fresh fruit as a topping. Fruit juice is not recommended during yeast cleanses.

Molasses is a great sweetener with a very distinctive taste. Most people will associate its unique aroma with gingerbread. Because of its very strong flavour, I recommend molasses mostly for heavier cakes and cookies, or in recipes calling for brown sugar. You won't want to use molasses in a white vanilla cake, for example, but it can work in a fruit cake or chocolate cake.

You will notice that I have not listed any artificial sweeteners. I won't go into detail on these products (aspartame, sucralose, malitol etc). Suffice it to say that I never use them myself and never feed them to any of my guests.

Substitution Example

Let's come back again to our chocolate chip cookie recipe and take it one step further to make it gluten-free, dairy-free and also sugar-free.

Modified Chocolate Chip Cookies (Gluten-Free and Dairy-Free)
from page 34

3/4 cup	Sugar	2 cups	Brown rice flour
3/4 cup	Brown sugar	3/4 cup	Tapioca starch
3/4 cup	Grapeseed oil	1 tsp	Baking soda
2	Eggs	3/4 tsp	Salt
1 tsp	Vanilla extract	2 cups	Chocolate chips*

*Dairy-free

Our refined sugars in the recipe are white sugar and brown sugar. In total, these two add up to 1-1/2 cups. We have many options here, but let's make a very straight forward substitution by using honey and molasses. Since molasses has a very strong and powerful flavour, we'll only use a small amount of it to imitate the flavour of brown sugar. To substitute for the remaining sweetness in this recipe, we'll use honey.

To replace the first cup of sugar, we'll use 3/4 cup of honey. And, for the additional 1/2 cup of sugar left in the original recipe, we'll use 1/4 cup of molasses. Our sweeteners now add up to the equivalent of our original 1-1/2 cups of white and brown sugar. Since we are now using 1 cup of liquid ingredients (honey and molasses) in place of a dry ingredient (sugar), let's also add another 1/2 cup of brown rice flour. Our recipe now becomes this:

Modified Chocolate Chip Cookies
(Gluten-Free, Dairy-Free and Sugar-Free)

3/4 cup	Honey	2-1/2 cups	Brown rice flour
1/4 cup	Molasses	3/4 cup	Tapioca starch
3/4 cup	Grapeseed oil	1 tsp	Baking soda
2	Eggs	3/4 tsp	Salt
1 tsp	Vanilla extract	2 cups	Chocolate chips*

*Dairy-free and unsweetened

Honey can burn easily in the oven, so for best results, you'll want to bake these on either an insulated cookie sheet or on a parchment lined cookie sheet. You can also substitute the sugar in this recipe with any combination of honey, stevia, agave nectar or xylitol. And, if you weren't able to find dairy-free, unsweetened chocolate chips, you can use raisins (with no added sugar) or nuts instead.

SOY

Soy is commonly grown as a rotational crop to corn, which is why it is a very prevalent food crop in North America. Coincidentally, as with corn, soy also happens to be a common food allergen. A dietician once told me that certain food sensitivities can be very dynamic, and can even change every 6 months. And, the more you eat a food, the more likely you are to become sensitized to it. With soy being so pervasive in processed foods, this argument might explain why so many people are intolerant to it (along with wheat, dairy and corn). Some symptoms associated with soy intolerance may include gas, bloating and other digestive complaints.

As discussed earlier in the dairy section, soy's isoflavones and phytoestrogens can be beneficial to some women due to their estrogenic effects. Soy can also be a great source of protein, but like anything else, should be enjoyed in moderation. If you can tolerate soy, try looking for certified organic varieties.

Commonly found in:
Soy milk, soy cheese or soy ice cream
Soybeans or edamame
Tofu
Soy oil
High protein bars and snacks
Margarine

Look out for:
Textured soy flour/protein
Textured vegetable protein
Vegetable shortening
Processed or mock meats

Hidden sources:
Baby formulas
Baked goods and baking mixes
Bread crumbs, breaded foods, cereals, crackers
Canned meat
Chewing gum
Chilli, pasta, stew
Cooking spray

Diet drinks and drink mixes
Frozen desserts
Hydrolyzed plant/soy/vegetable protein
Lecithin
Mixed seasonings, spices
Monosodium glutamate (MSG)
Peanut butter
Prepared soups
Processed sauces
Salad dressings, gravies, sauces
Snack foods
Spreads, dips, mayonnaise
Thickening agents
Vegetable shortening, vegetable oil
Vegetarian dishes

Non-food sources of soy:
Cosmetics, soaps
Craft materials
Glycerine
Some vitamins and medications

Substitutions

Make sure you read product labels carefully to avoid products that contain soy and soy derivatives. Avoid food and products that do not have an ingredient list and read labels every time you shop.

When cooking, the most important thing to do is to look for hidden soy in your ingredients. For obvious additions of soy, simply substitute soy milk with any other milk alternative listed in the Dairy section, omit tofu and replace mock and deli meats with the real thing. If you are a vegetarian, try substituting tofu with the other many protein rich options available to you such as legumes and quinoa.

CORN

According to Agriculture and Agri-Food Canada, corn accounts for over 70% of the world's coarse grain market, which helps explain why it can be found in a huge variety of foods today. What's also interesting to note is that according to Statistics Canada, 57% of the area devoted to growing corn in Canada during 2008-2009 was planted with genetically modified seeds.

Corn and its derivatives can be found almost everywhere – from tacos to chewing gum, from milk carton linings to cosmetics, and from plastics to glues. And because it's so abundantly available and cheap, it is often used to feed farm animals that really have no business eating grains in the first place. The story of corn is fascinating and eye opening. If you're interested in finding more about corn and where your food comes from, I highly recommend reading Michael Polan's *The Omnivore's Dilemma*.

Commonly found in:
Cakes, cookies and candies
Corn starch
Corn syrup or high fructose corn syrup (HFCS)
Cornmeal
Ketchup and liquid mustard
Malt, malt syrup or malt extract
Margarine
Popcorn
Pre-packaged frozen meals
Prepared sauces and salad dressings
Refined sugars
Tacos and corn chips
Vinegar
Vitamins, supplements and prescription drugs

Look out for:
Dextrose
Fructose
Fruit sugar
Sucrose
Sorbitol

Hidden sources:
Baby food
Baking powder
Cake frostings
Canned vegetables (in corn vinegar)
Cereal
Chewing gum
Chips
Confectioner's sugar (icing sugar)
Enriched milk and flour
Fried foods (when fried in soy oil)
Ice cream
Jam
Liquorice
Marshmallows
Peanut butter
Prepared Chinese dishes (thickened with corn starch)
Processed meats
Wax coatings on some fresh fruit and vegetables
Whiskey
Yeast
Yogurt

Non-food sources of corn:
Adhesives and glues including envelope and stamp glue
Cosmetics and shaving foams
Crayons and chalk
Disposable paper plates and cups
Ethanol fuel
Milk carton linings
Paperboard
Plastic wrap
Soaps
Toothpaste

Substitutions
Because of its prevalence in even things like the stamps that you lick, avoiding corn is very challenging. Read labels very carefully, and con-

sider the type of packaging that you are buying – even cartons can be lined with corn products.

Substituting for corn can be tricky but here are a few tips:

Corn product	Substitute
Baking powder	Combine baking soda, cream of tartar and tapioca starch in a ratio of 1:2:1
Cereal	Cream of rice, rice/quinoa/oat flakes
Confectioner's sugar	Combine 1 cup xylitol or white sugar with 1 tbsp tapioca starch or arrowroot flour. Pulse in blender until it becomes a fine powder.
Corn based sugars	Honey, maple syrup, stevia (see Sugar section)
Corn oil	Grapeseed oil
Corn starch	Tapioca starch or arrowroot flour
Cornmeal	Millet flour
Malt syrup or corn syrup	Brown rice syrup
Tacos	Soft rice wraps or lettuce leaves
Vinegar	Lemon juice
Carton beverages	Beverages packaged in plastic or glass containers

TROUBLESHOOTING GUIDE

Knowing how to replace wheat/gluten, dairy, sugar, soy and corn is essential to being able to modify recipes to your specific dietary needs. But what we've discussed so far is really only half of the puzzle. As we discussed earlier, making substitutions is not an exact science and the previous substitution charts are only general guidelines. In order to make truly successful substitutions, you also need to know how to troubleshoot your baked goods and fix them if they don't turn out exactly as you had hoped.

Before we get into the details of troubleshooting recipes, I want to re-emphasize the most basic principle of making substitutions: always try to maintain the total proportion of dry ingredients to wet ingredients. For example, you can substitute 1 cup of quinoa with 1 cup of rice; 1 pound of ground beef with 1 pound of crumbled tofu; 1 cup of wheat flour with 1 cup of gluten-free flours; or 1 cup of corn syrup with 1 cup of rice syrup.

If, for some reason, you end up substituting a wet ingredient for a dry one, you will have to compensate for the difference. Just as we discussed in the sugar and dairy substitution sections, you can compensate for added wet ingredients by either omitting the same amount of liquid elsewhere in the recipe, or by adding dry ingredients equal to about half the wet ingredient's volume (e.g. add 1/2 cup of flour for every 1 cup of honey). What you're ultimately trying to do is maintain the texture of the original recipe.

How do you know what texture a batter should be? Well, if you've made the recipe before, hopefully you'll have a general idea of what it should look and feel like. But even if you don't, look for clues in your recipe's instructions. If it says to "pour" batter into a pan, then your batter should be pourable like yogurt or thick melted chocolate. If it says to "spread evenly" into a pan, then it should be thick enough that it retains its own shape and requires you to spread it around with a spoon like soft cream cheese or sour cream.

If your batter is too thick – add more liquid a tablespoon at a time and mix well. And if it's too runny, add more flour. Don't be afraid to add and subtract from recipes that you need to modify. (Check the Troubleshooting chart on the next page for more help.) To make things easier the next time around, always keep a running tally of all the changes you've made to a recipe. If your food turns out to be a masterpiece, you'll be able to do it again without the guess-work. Once you get the hang of substituting and troubleshooting, it should only take you one or two tries to get things right.

Making mistakes is just a natural part of learning how to cook with unfamiliar foods. So don't be angry or disappointed when mistakes happen. Instead, treat the situation like a doctor treats a sick patient: diagnose, prescribe, treat and revisit. Use the chart on the following page to diagnose common problems with baked goods and figure out how to fix them. As long as you have written down exactly what you've done to change a recipe, you can always work out any further changes on paper before trying the recipe again.

Problem	Reason	Recommended fix for 8" cake, bread loaf or 2 dozen cupcakes
Cooked on the outside and raw or soggy in the middle	Not cooked long enough; OR Too much fat content OR Baking pan is too big	Return to oven and check every 5 minutes. If middle remains soggy despite a long cooking time, there is too much fat. Cut 1/4 to 1/2 cup oil from recipe. If problem persists, add 1/2 cup flours as well and/or try using a smaller baking pan.
Too dry	Not enough fat content	Add 1/4 cup oil, OR Add 1 egg and reduce water/milk by 1 cup
Too crumbly	Not enough binding aids	Add 2 tbsp psyllium husks and 1/4 cup water; OR Add 1 egg and 3/4 to 1 cup flour OR Add 1/4 – 1/2 cup tapioca flour (or other binding aid), reduce bulk flour by same amount
Too tough or chewy (cake)	Too much binding aid	Reduce 1/4 – 1/2 cup binding aid, increase bulk flour by same amount
Didn't rise enough, too dense	Not enough leavening aids	Add 1 tbsp baking powder; AND/OR Add 1 egg and 1/2 cup flour
Too tough or chewy (crust/crackers)	Not enough leavening aids	Add 1 tbsp baking powder; AND/OR Add 1 egg and 3/4 - 1 cup flour
Started to burn early in oven	Too much sugar content	If using maple syrup, reduce amount used and substitute honey or stevia
Caused an adverse reaction	Contamination	Check all labels carefully. Call manufacturers if in doubt. Check for and eliminate contamination sources.

You can find the metric version of this table on page 167

CHAPTER 4:
ENJOY A VARIETY OF FOODS

How many times have you stood staring at your open fridge trying to figure out what to make for dinner? Knowing how to substitute for wheat, dairy, sugar, soy and corn is invaluable in managing food sensitivities. But to truly be dynamic, you should also know how to substitute vegetables, grains and meats when either you or the store doesn't have exactly what you need.

GRAINS

The easiest way to prepare grains is with a rice cooker, which can be found in most kitchen appliance sections, in Asian markets and on the Internet. I use a rice cooker with an uncoated stainless steel interior (which was not very easy to find). When purchasing a rice cooker, try to select one that includes an optional steaming basket so that you can steam your veggies at the same time.

White rice is an easy place to start. It is a mild flavoured grain that can complement virtually any dish. I grew up eating white jasmine scented rice, but eventually switched to brown rice for its superior fibre and nutritional content. In the refinement process, white rice looses two thirds of its vitamins, two thirds of its fibre and half its minerals. Still, white rice is nice on occasion, especially when it is cooked with saffron, tumeric or coconut. Rice does tend to be treated heavily with pesticides and fungicides, and is often coated with talc. So choose certified organic rice, especially if you are eating it every day, and wash it well before cooking.

Brown rice does take much longer to cook than white rice, but this can be shortened if pre-soaked. Brown rice needs slightly more water than white rice to cook. Once the grains have begun to split open, they have finished cooking.

Wild rice is a longer, crunchier and much darker grain than white or brown rice. It has a much more distinctive flavour to it than brown or white rice, and is generally very expensive. Wild rice is normally prepared mixed sparingly with white or brown rice.

Quinoa is another alternative grain. Nutty and fragrant, quinoa is beige coloured, small, round and very light weight. You may also find red quinoa which is deep red-brown in colour, slightly more fragrant and nutty, but equally delicate in flavour. Quinoa is an ancient grain originating from the Andes in South America where it was once a staple food for the Incans. This gluten-free grain is the most high in amino acids of all grains and can be an adequate protein substitute for vegetarians. It is also a good source of fibre, complex carbohydrates, calcium, phosphorous, iron and vitamins B and E. Quinoa cooks faster than rice, so is a great choice when you're pinched for time.

Millet is a yellow grain that looks much like quinoa. Cooked just right, it comes out light and fluffy. Millet also makes a great hot breakfast cereal when mixed with nuts and fruit. Unlike the other grains discussed earlier, millet is an alkaline forming food, and a great choice for individuals that need to lower their internal acidity.

Buckwheat (Kasha) is a dark brown tear-drop shaped seed that, despite its name, is not related to wheat and is gluten-free. Originating in Asia, buckwheat is grown around the world today, but is still relatively unappreciated. It is a great source of protein, with a complete amino acid profile, and also contains vitamins E and B. Like millet, this grain is also alkaline forming. Buckwheat groats, or Kasha, can be cooked and enjoyed like rice. Buckwheat flour can also be used to bake, and is often used to make pancakes and Japanese soba noodles.

VEGETABLES

Let's first talk about getting the most from your vegetables. When picking vegetables, the general rule of thumb is to look for deeply coloured and firm items. Avoid vegetables that show signs of age, like mould on ends/tips, limp or yellowing leaves, or relatively dull colours. You can also examine the underside of stemmed vegetables, like broccoli and asparagus, that will crack from the bottom as they age. And before cooking or eating raw, always rinse your vegetables well. A sieve or salad spinner will be invaluable if you plan on enjoying plenty of raw leafy greens.

To extend the life of your vegetables and help preserve their nutritional value, here are a few easy tips to follow:

- Buy local and/or organic vegetables when they are in season
- Enjoy raw when possible
- Store in closed containers or bags in the refrigerator (except for tomatoes, potatoes and onions which should be kept at room temperature)
- Minimize exposure to heat and water by steaming, baking at low temperatures, or boiling in small amounts of water
- Cover exposed cut surfaces before storing

In previous sections of this book, we've discussed substitutions for wheat, dairy, soy, corn and grains. Knowing how to substitute vegetables can be equally as handy, especially if you're preparing a recipe with a limited selection in your fridge. Vegetables can be grouped together very simply, and within these groups, you can generally make easy, straight substitutions. These groups are: leafy and salad vegetables; fruits; squashes and melons; flowers and flower buds; podded vegetables; bulb and stem vegetables; and root and tuberous vegetables. Below are lists of a number of common and not-so-common vegetables in each group, along with preparation tips and nutritional information.

Leafy And Salad Vegetables

Amaranth (Bayam or Kulitis) – Use in soups or stir fries. High in vitamins, minerals and oxalic acid. Seeds produce a high protein grain. Traditionally used in Africa to treat low red blood cell count.

Arugula – Enjoy cooked or raw. Mild flavoured leafy green. Good substitute for spinach. Rich in vitamin C and potassium. Considered an aphrodisiac by ancient Romans.

Beet greens – Steam young leaves briefly or enjoy as a salad. Enjoy older leaves in stir fries. Beet greens belong to the amaranth family and are also related to chard.

Bitterleaf (Ironweed) – Sweet and bitter taste, commonly used in soups. Found in African grocery stores. Medicinal plant traditionally used for diabetes, fever, headache, joint pain, gingivitis and toothache. Also traditionally used as a uterus toner and blood purifier. Contains sesquiterpene lactone that may have anti-inflammatory and anti-cancer effects according to the U.S. National Cancer Institute.

Bok choy – Rinse thoroughly and steam briefly or boil. Great for noodle soups. Light in flavour. Related to western cabbage and turnip.

Brussels sprout – Cut off and discard stem. Boil, steam or roast – do not overcook. High in vitamins A and C, folic acid and fibre.

Cabbage – Slice thinly and boil for 4 minutes. Overcooking may release strong odours. Best for soups, stews or cabbage rolls. Preserved as kimchi or sauerkraut. Source of riboflavin, vitamin C and glutamine (anti-inflammatory).

Chard (Swiss chard, Silverbeet, Spinach beet or Mangold) – Eat young leaves raw in salads. Older leaves can be steamed or sautéed. Slightly bitter taste improves with cooking. Delicate substitute for spinach or arugula. Green ribbed leaves come with various coloured stems.

Chinese cabbage (Nappa cabbage) – Mild tasting light coloured leaves, best enjoyed sliced and boiled in soups. Also used to make kimchi. Can also be used as an edible lining to steaming baskets. Source of beta carotene, vitamins A and C.

Chrysanthemum leaves – Leaves can be steamed or boiled. Dried flowers are often used to make sweet chrysanthemum tea. Traditionally used to help treat influenza. Seeds are used to produce insecticides and can repel insects.

Collard greens (Couve or Kovi) – Slice thinly and sauté. Enjoy with beans or meats. Good substitute or compliment to kale, spinach and mustard greens. Good source of vitamin C and fibre.

Corn salad (Lewiston cornsalad, Lamb's lettuce, Field salad, or Rapunzel) – Small leafy plant can be enjoyed raw or steamed. High in vitamins C, B6, B9, E, beta carotene, and omega-3 fatty acids.

Cress – Peppery and tangy flavour great for soups, sandwiches and salads. Can also be eaten as sprouts.

Dandelion – Eat raw as a salad or sautéed. High in vitamins A, C, K, calcium, potassium, beta carotene iron and manganese. Used in traditional Chinese medicine for liver detoxification, as a diuretic and to reduce inflammation.

Endive (Belgian endive, French endive, Witlof) – Cut and discard hard inner part of stem before cooking. Eat raw, baked, boiled or stuffed. This small, cream-coloured head is grown in the absence of light to maintain its white leaves, and reduce its naturally bitter flavour.

Epazote (Wormseed, Jesuit's tea, Mexican tea or Herba sancti) – Use as flavouring for black beans and Mexican dishes such as quesadillas, sopes, and enchiladas. Strong flavoured herb similar to anise, fennel and tarragon. Used traditionally to prevent flatulence, amenorrhea, dysmenorrhoea, hysteria, asthma and intestinal worms.

Fat hen (White goosefoot) – Eat young leaves as a salad, or steamed like spinach. Black seeds are high in protein, vitamin A, calcium, phosphorus and potassium. High in oxalic acid. Closely related to quinoa.

Fiddlehead – Steam, boil or sauté until crisp tender. Fiddleheads are the unfurled leaves of developing ferns, and are only available in the spring. Enjoy in sparse moderation. May contain thiaminase which breaks down thiamine.

Gailan (Chinese broccoli) – Can be stir fried with ginger and garlic, boiled or steamed. Usually served with oyster sauce, although this sauce is typically not gluten-free. Slightly sweeter than broccoli. Leaves, stems and yellow flowers can all be eaten.

Garden rocket – Rich, peppery leaves can be enjoyed as salad, or cooked with pasta sauces or meats. High in vitamin C and potassium.

Kale – Best enjoyed when sliced thinly and sautéed or steamed. Antioxidant and anti-inflammatory. High in beta carotene, vitamins K and C, lutein, zeaxanthin and calcium. Reduce bitterness and increase sweetness by freezing before cooking.

Lettuce – Eat raw as salad or in sandwiches and wraps. Comes in many varieties: butterhead, iceburg, romaine, Boston, summer crisp and more. Source of vitamin A and folic acid.

Mustard leaves – Raw leaves add a spicy flavour to salads. Can also be boiled or steamed. Substitute for arugula, spinach or tatsoi.

Radicchio (Red endive, Red chicory) – Bitter and spicy taste becomes more mild when grilled or roasted. Can also be used in salads to add colour with its red or red/green leaves.

Rapini (Broccoli rabe or Raab) – Steam or stir fry; good substitute for broccoli. Some may have small edible flowers. Source of vitamins A, C and K, potassium, calcium and iron.

Sorrel (Garden sorrel or Commen sorrel) – Purée leaves in soups and sauces, or add to salads. Ascorbic acid content imparts a flavour similar to kiwi or sour strawberries.

Spinach – Best eaten raw, or quickly steamed. Rich in vitamins A, C, E and K, magnesium, manganese, folate, iron and calcium, but high in oxalic acid.

Tatsoi (Spinach mustard, Spoon mustard, Rosette bok choy) – Best eaten raw in salads. Also great in soups, sautéed, boiled or steamed, served with chicken, tofu or seafood. Similar texture to bok choy with a stronger spicy flavour.

Turnip greens – Eat raw in salads, sautéed or in soups. Good substitute for spinach. Good source of vitamins A, C and K, folate, calcium and lutein. Traditionally used to relieve symptoms of rheumatoid arthritis, and atherosclerosis, and to help promote colon and lung health.

Watercress (Indian cress) – Best steamed or in soups. Leaves will become bitter as the plant flowers. High in vitamins A and C, iron, calcium, iodine and folic acid. May have anticancer effects according to the U.S. National Cancer Institute.

Yarrow – Brew flowers for tea. Raw leaves can be chewed to help relieve toothaches. Traditionally used to treat various blood related conditions, slow bleeding from wounds, speed recovery from bruising and treat inflammation causing haemorrhoids and headaches.

Fruits (Excluding Squashes And Melons)

Avocado – Best eaten raw in salads, sandwiches or dips. Fruit is ripe when skin turns black and fruit is slightly tender. High monounsaturated fat content makes it a good source of fat for vegetarians. Also high in fibre, potassium and vitamins B, E and K.

Bell pepper – Eat raw in salads, steamed or sautéed. Choose certified organic varieties as these tend to be treated heavily with pesticides. Part of the nightshade family.

Chayote – Eat raw in salads, boiled, stuffed, mashed, baked or sautéed (skin can be eaten). Substitute for cucumber or potato. Resembles a coarsely wrinkled green pear.

Chili pepper – Eat raw or cooked in salads or recipes to add heat. Hot flavour is mostly concentrated in stem and white flesh surrounding seeds. Use or discard these parts depending on desired flavour. Handle with care, do not touch eyes.

Cucumber – Slice thinly into circles or long sticks. Enjoy raw in salads, sandwiches or as a healthy snack. English cucumbers do not need to be peeled.

Sweet corn – Best boiled or roasted on the cob. Common allergen.

Tomato – Eat raw in salads or hors d'oeuvres, cooked in soups and sauces, roasted or stuffed. Lends flavour when sautéed with other vegetables. Choose certified organic varieties when available. High in licopene. Part of the nightshade family.

Squashes And Melons

Acorn squash – Inner flesh can be eaten baked, sautéed or steamed. Seeds can be toasted and eaten as well. Looks like a small green pumpkin. High in beta caroene, fibre, potassium, magnesium, manganese and vitamins C and B.

Bitter melon – Slice in half and discard seeds. Slice remaining melon thinly and cook by frying, steaming or boiling in soup. Melon becomes more bitter as it ripens so it is usually eaten while still green. Looks like a warty cucumber. A 2008 study from the Garvan Institute of Medical Research and the Shanghai Institute of Materia Medica showed that bitter melon can be beneficial to diabetics by enabling glucose uptake.

Eggplant (Aubergine) – Best in stews, roasted, or stuffed. Naturally bitter taste improves when cooked. Most commonly found as a dark purple variety, also grows in white, yellow and green. Good source of folic acid and potassium. Part of the nightshade family.

Pumpkin – Flesh can be boiled, baked, steamed or roasted. Delicate sweet taste is great mashed, or in soups and pies. Seeds can be roasted and eaten. A 2007 study in China showed eating pumpkin helped promote regeneration of damaged pancreatic cells.

Winter melon – Inner flesh can be cubed and boiled in soup with pork or beef. Sometimes also used in curries. Mild tasting flesh becomes translucent when cooked. Look for this melon in Asian grocery stores. Looks like a round or oval honeydew with smooth and slightly mottled green skin.

Zucchini (Courgette) – Can be eaten raw, but best served steamed, boiled, grilled, stuffed or baked. Season lightly to enjoy its delicate flavour. Can also be grated and baked into breads or cakes. High in folate, potassium, vitamin A and manganese.

Flowers And Flower Buds

Artichoke – Best steamed or boiled until tender. Can be eaten on its own, cooked with other vegetables, or served cold in salads. Hearts can also be added to salads or bakes. Eat only the soft bottom parts of leaves and tender heart (middle). Discard hard sections of leaves and fuzzy centre. Shown to help reduce blood cholesterol levels.

Broccoli – Best steamed or boiled until stalk can be easily pierced with a knife. Plunge cooked broccoli into cold water to help it maintain a bright green colour. Can also be eaten raw as a snack. High in fibre and vitamins C, K and A, with small amounts of selenium.

Cauliflower – Remove outer green leaves and stalk. Steam or boil until base can be easily pierced with a knife. Can be eaten raw as a snack. Boil leaves and stalk to make vegetable broth before discarding. High in vitamin C, fibre and folate.

Podded Vegetables

Azuki bean (Adzuki or Red bean) – Commonly used in Asian cuisine as a sweetened paste filling, in sweet soups, or as a topping over shaved ice. The small red bean can also sometimes be found in white, black, grey or mottled varieties.

Black-eyed pea – Most often enjoyed in southern soul food cuisine, accompanying pork (bacon, ham bones, or fatback), onion and hot sauce. Medium sized pale coloured bean with a black spot tradition-ally believed to bring prosperity when eaten on New Year's Day.

Chickpea (Garbonzo bean, Indian pea, Kabuli chana) – Boil until tender and serve with salad, in stew or chilli. Chickpea flour can be made into falafels, or used as a thickening agent. Ground chickpeas can also be made into hummus. High protein legume is great for vegetarians. Soak dried chickpeas 12-24 hours to reduce cooking time.

Fava bean (Broad, Field, Bell or Tic bean) – Can be eaten in a vari-ety of ways, but should always be cooked. Enjoy fried and spiced as a savoury snack, mashed and used as filling in wraps, or boiled whole in vegetable soups.

Green bean (French String or Runner bean) – Discard stems before boiling, steaming or frying. Makes an excellent side dish and can be added to stir fries. Good source of vitamins A and C.

Guar bean (Cluster bean) – Can be eaten as a green bean, but most commonly used to extract guar gum. Use guar gum as a thickening agent for dairy products (yogurt, ice cream, cheese) or baked goods.

Lentil (Daal or Dal) – Boil to make soups, or cook together with rice. Can also be combined with vegetables for a protein-rich vegetar-ian dish. Sprouted lentils are more complete in amino acids. This leg-ume is also high in fibre, folate, vitamin B1, iron and minerals.

Lima Bean (Butter, Sugar or Haba bean) – Always cook by boiling before eating. Can be added to soups, salads or stews. High in fibre, protein and iron.

Mung bean – Most often cooked in Asian cuisine as a sweet soup by boiling in water with sugar. Cooked beans can also be puréed and sweetened to make a sweet paste filling similar to red bean paste. Prepared in Indian cuisine with sugar, coconut milk and ginger. Sprouted mung beans are usually simply called "bean sprouts". Sprouts can be cooked in stir fries, or served raw with Vietnamese soup noodles.

Okra (Lady's fingers) – Stir fry with spices of choice, or add as a thickening agent for soup, stew and gumbo. Stir frying will help remove moisture and reduce sliminess. Also used in many Indian vegetable dishes. Use leaves as a substitute for dandelion or beet greens, or enjoy raw in salads. High in fibre, protein, calcium, vitamins A and B.

Pea – Boil fresh peas to achieve a sweeter taste. Fresh peas can be spiced and served as a side, or added to various dishes like noodles, stir fries, casseroles or pot pies. Dried peas can be cooked in soups. While often served only for their inner seeds, young and tender pea pods can be eaten whole.

Soybean (Soya bean or Edamame) – Always boil or steam, do not eat raw. Complete protein profile is beneficial for vegetarians, but it is also a common allergen found in many processed foods.

Yardlong bean (Snake bean or Chinese long bean) – Can be eaten fresh or cooked, best chosen when young and slender. Cook in stir fries or cooked salads. Good substitute for green beans. Good source of protein, vitamins A and C, folate and various minerals.

Bulb And Stem Vegetables

Asparagus – Boil or steam vegetable either chopped or whole. Can also be grilled, baked or added to stir fries. Choose young shoots in the spring. Holes or cracks on the underside of shoots is an indication of age. Good source of folic acid, potassium, antioxidants and fibre. May cause odorous urine.

Celery – Eat stalks raw, steamed or stir fried. High in fibre, low in calories. Seeds can be used as a flavouring spice. Fleshy root can also be cooked like a turnip. Choose certified organic when possible.

Garlic – Remove papery skin and chop, mince, slice or press. Use whole in slow cooker recipes. Add to virtually any dish to add flavour. Spiciness is reduced with longer cooking times or by removing the bulb's centre. Can also be sliced and roasted to use on pizzas or appetizers. A 2001 study from the University of Wales examined garlic's antibacterial, antiviral, antifungal and antiprotozoal activity.

Kohlrabi – Cut in sections and boil or steam. Leaves can also be cooked and eaten. Good substitute for broccoli, cauliflower or cabbage hearts.

Fennel – Very aromatic and flavourful bulb, leaves and seeds, similar in taste to anise (liquorice). Eat bulb and leaves raw or cooked in sides, salads or pastas. Can also be sliced and roasted, or added to vegetable medleys and risotto. Use dried green seeds as a cooking spice for sausages and meatballs. Delicate dill-like leaves can be sprinkled over salads. Fennel, like soy, contains phytoestrogens which may be beneficial to some women. Fennel syrup has been traditionally used to help relieve coughs, while powdered fennel has been traditionally used to help repel fleas.

Leek – Best sliced finely and cooked similarly to onions. Both the white base and green stems are edible and share a similar flavour, although the base is stronger in flavour. Very similar taste to garlic and onion. White base section is a good substitute for onions in most recipes. Also a great addition to vegetable soups. Wash carefully before and after cutting, as dirt can hide in between bunched leaves.

Root And Tuberous Vegetables

Bamboo shoot – Most commonly found canned, only the soft inner flesh is edible. Slice thinly and boil or sauté to cook. Fresh shoots must be boiled in large amounts of water to reduce potential toxicity. (Water used to boil shoots should be discarded.) Indonesian recipes cook bamboo shoots in coconut milk and spices. Very distinctive earthy flavour compliments shitake or oyster mushrooms, pork and stir fries.

Beetroot (Garden beet) – Peel, slice and steam. Enjoy alone, with butter, cubed in salads or pickled. Can also be used to make beet soup (borscht). Beetroot powder or juice can be used as a natural red food colouring. According to a Hungarian study conducted in 2007, beetroot can be beneficial for the liver. Beetroot can also help reduce blood pressure according to the American Heart Association.

Burdock root (Gobo) – Soak root in water 5-10 minutes before cooking to reduce muddy flavour. Bake with garlic and spices or with other root vegetables. Can also be added to chilli, or boiled to make soup/tea. Traditionally used by herbalists as a diuretic, diaphoretic, and blood purifying agent. Good source of minerals, thiamine, inulin and vitamin C. This plant is best known for its prickly "burrs" that attach onto clothing and pet fur.

Carrot – Peel and enjoy raw, juiced, or cooked in soups or stews. Can also be roasted, boiled, steamed, or baked into carrot cake. High in fibre, beta carotene, minerals and antioxidants.

Cassava (Yuca or Manioc) – Boil, bake or deep fry. Do not eat raw. Good substitute for potatoes in stews or for fries/chips. Starchy root flour is known as tapioca flour or tapioca starch. Tapioca pearls can be made into puddings or other desserts while tapioca starch is used as a binding aid in gluten-free cooking. High in calcium, phosphorus and vitamin C.

Chicory (Radicchio, Sugarloaf, Belgian endive) – Root may be ground and used as coffee substitute. Also found in fibre supplements (inulin). Traditionally used to treat gallstones, gastro-enteritis, sinus problems, cuts and bruises and to stimulate appetite. See Radicchio and Endive in previous Leafy and Salad Vegetables section.

Daikon (Chinese radish or Lobok) – Most often pickled, or shredded and cooked into a custard-like dim sum dish in Chinese cuisine. Can be very odorous when cooked, but yields a mild and pleasant taste.

Ginger – Peel, slice and add to various dishes as a flavouring spice in foods. Can also be boiled into a tea with honey or pickled. Traditionally used to treat motion sickness and nausea. Also traditionally used to stimulate the gastrointestinal tract, as a cold remedy and as an analgesic.

Lotus root – Flowers, seeds, young leaves and roots can all be eaten but should always be cooked. Tender leaves can be used as garnish in Asian cuisine, while older leaves are used to wrap foods to make sticky rice bundles generally served at dim sum. Crunchy and tangy roots can be pickled, cooked in soups, or boiled and eaten as a snack or accompaniment. Stamens can be dried and made into tea. Seeds can be eaten raw, dried and popped, or cooked into lotus seed paste which can be used as pastry filling in Asian desserts.

Onion – Remove papery skin before cooking. Can be chopped, sliced or diced, and roasted, steamed, stewed or sautéed. Excellent natural flavour enhancer for vegetables and meats.

Shallot – Remove and discard papery skin before cooking. Very similar in taste to onions, but slightly milder and sweeter. Can be used in place of onions, or added to recipes to enhance flavour. Grows in clustered cloves similar to garlic but usually larger.

Parsnip – Peel, chop or slice, and roast or boil. Can also be added to soups, stews and casseroles. Good substitute for potatoes or carrots.

Potato – Potatoes can be enjoyed in soups, stews or casseroles; mashed, baked or deep fried. "Eyes" should be removed before cooking, although skin can be eaten if well cleaned. High in vitamins C and B6, potassium, and various minerals. Part of the nightshade family. Substitute potato with cassava root, yams, sweet potato, taro or burdock root.

Radish – Root can be sliced and eaten raw in salads to add a spicy and peppery taste. Can also be peeled and boiled until tender with dried scallops to make a delicate side dish. Leaves are edible. Traditionally used to help relieve coughs, gastric discomfort, kidney stones and parasites.

Rutabaga root (Yellow turnip) – Peel and add to stews, casseroles or soups. Can also be mashed, or roasted with meat dishes or other root vegetables. Leaf stalks can also be cooked and made into rutabaga jam or pie.

Sweet potato – Peel then boil, bake, or fry in similar manner as common potatoes. Can be mashed, added to stews, soups or casseroles. Cook in sweet soups with taro, red beans and/or tapioca pearls. More nutritious than the common potato, sweet potatoes are rich in complex carbohydrates, fibre, beta carotene, and vitamins C and B6. This vegetable has a deep orange flesh.

Taro – Peel and boil or bake. Best enjoyed alongside pork or duck. Can also be mashed, or cubed and boiled in sweet soups. High in calcium oxalate, which can be reduced through cooking or soaking overnight. Substitute with potatoes, sweet potatoes or yams.

Turnip – Peel, slice and bake with oil and spices. Great addition to root vegetable bakes. Can also be sliced thinly and fried into chips. Turnip greens can be eaten as a leafy vegetable and substituted for mustard greens.

Water chestnut – Peel and enjoy raw, boiled, grilled or pickled. Light and crispy in flavour, this is a great vegetable to add to dishes for a crunchy texture. Good source of carbohydrates, fibre, vitamin B6, potassium, copper and manganese.

Yam – Peel and boil, bake or fry. Pale white to yellow flesh turns purple or pink as it ripens. Good substitute for sweet potatoes, common potatoes, or taro. High in vitamins C and B6, fibre, potassium and manganese.

MEATS

Enjoying a variety of different high quality meats can be easier than you think. Most recipes lend themselves very well to substituting meats, especially if you are substituting within the same group of meats. And while you should feel free to experiment with flavours – I have included generally complimentary spices for each group of meats below.

Grouping	Meats	Complimentary Flavours
Red meats	Beef	Wheat-free tamari sauce
	Venison	Rosemary
	Caribou	Mustard powder
	Ostrich	Bay leaf
	Duck	Basil
	Sheep	Garlic
		Sea salt / pepper
White meats	Chicken	Thyme
	Turkey	Oregano
	Pork	Bay leaf
	Boar	Dill
	Frog	Garlic
	Rabbit	Sea salt / pepper
	Veal	Mint
	Lamb	
Shellfish	Shrimp	Bay leaf
	Crawfish	Sage
	Lobster	Worchester sauce*
	Crab	Wheat-free tamari sauce
	Scallops	Garlic
	Mussels	Sea salt / pepper
	Clams	
	Oysters	

not gluten-free

White fish	Tilapia	Thyme
	Cod	Sage
	Bass	Garlic
	Halibut	Sea salt / pepper
Dark or fatty fish	Salmon	Oregano
	Rainbow trout	Basil
	Tuna	Garlic
		Sea salt / pepper

The list above is by no means complete, but should give you a good idea of where most meats can fall. Store a variety of meats and spices from each of the groups listed above so that you'll always have something on hand to satisfy a sudden craving.

Wild game is often accused of tasting "gamey" and having a very strong meaty flavour. But this flavour comes less from the animal itself, and more from what the animal *eats*. One of my local farmers told me that tree bark is the main culprit for this distinctive flavour. So if you prefer milder tasting game, find a farmer at your local market that raises their animals on grass, and limits access to bark. In general, wild game also tends to be much leaner. So, when substituting common meats for game, add some healthy fat such as olive oil (about 1 tbsp per pound of meat). This will help prevent the meat from tasting dry.

Fish is a wonderfully healthy source of protein, essential fatty acids and other nutrients. Due to pollution and environmental contamination, however, not all fish are safe to eat on a regular basis. The list below is from the *Consumer Guide to Mercury in Fish,* as published by the Natural Resources Defence Council. While this guide was created for pregnant (or soon to be pregnant) women, it is still useful for anyone looking to reduce their exposure to mercury. It also indicates over-fished species whose numbers are dwindling. For the complete guide and further information, visit:
www.nrdc.org/health/effects/mercury/guide.asp.

Least mercury (Enjoy as often as desired)

Anchovies

Clam

Crab (Domestic)

Crawfish/Crayfish

Haddock (Atlantic)*

Oyster

Perch (Ocean)

Salmon (Canned or Fresh)**

Sardine

Scallop*

Shrimp*

Sole (Pacific)

Squid (Calamari)

Tilapia

Trout (Freshwater)

Whitefish

Moderate mercury (Eat six servings or less per month)

Bass (Striped, Black)

Cod (Alaskan)*

Halibut (Atlantic)*

Halibut (Pacific)

Lobster

Snapper*

Tuna (Canned chunk light)

Tuna (Skipjack)*

High mercury (Eat three servings or less per month)

Bluefish

Grouper*

Mackerel (Spanish, Gulf)

Sea Bass (Chilean)*

Tuna (Canned Albacore)

Tuna (Yellowfin)*

Highest mercury (Avoid eating)

Mackerel (King)

Marlin*

Orange Roughy*

Shark*

Swordfish*

Tilefish*

Tuna (Bigeye, Ahi)*

* Fish in Trouble! These fish are perilously low in numbers or are caught using environmentally destructive methods.

** Farmed Salmon may contain PCB's, chemicals with serious long-term health effects.

The excerpt above has been republished, with permission, courtesy of the Natural Resources Defence Council.

CLOSING REMARKS

I hope that you have found this book informative and helpful so far, and that you find some recipes in the following pages to help you on your journey. I encourage you to keep this book handy and use it as a reference the next time you want to modify a recipe (old or new), or cook an unfamiliar grain, vegetable or meat. Don't be afraid to experiment, and by all means, scribble your own notes or substitutions directly into the recipes in this book.

Changing your diet to meet your new needs may not come easily at first – but what worthwhile changes in life are? Make a commitment to yourself to strict adherence for a month, and your changes will gradually become habits. Be patient, because once you develop these new habits, your food intolerances will open new doors for you and your long term health.

CHAPTER 5: RECIPES

SOUPS

Soups make great appetizers and are a great way to enjoy a variety of vegetables. They are easy to make and easy to store, which makes them great time savers overall. If you make a big batch of soup, you can store extra servings in glass jars in your refrigerator generally up to 1 week. For longer storage times, freeze extra soup in wide mouthed containers or in ice cube trays. Just remember that water expands when it freezes, so leave plenty of room in your containers so that they don't burst in your freezer.

BASIC BROTH 68

VEGETABLE BROTH 69

VEGETARIAN OKRA STEW 70

BUTTERNUT SQUASH SOUP 72

FRENCH ONION SOUP 73

TOMATO EGG-DROP SOUP 74

WINTER MELON WATERCRESS SOUP 75

BASIC BROTH

Most canned consommés – or clear soups like chicken or beef broth – contain a lot of salt, MSG and other ingredients that you may not want to eat. Fortunately, this is the easiest type of soup to make, and you can store it for quick use later on. Whenever you roast a chicken, turkey, beef or pork, keep the bones to make a batch of nutritious and flavourful broth.

I recommend freezing your stocks into ice cube trays. This way, you can thaw and use as little or as much as you want later on. In addition to using these as soups, small amounts of broth are great for adding flavour to a variety of dishes with grains and vegetables.

Ingredients:

24 oz	Water	3L
1/2 tsp	Sea salt	2.5ml
	Leftover bones from 1 chicken	
	OR	
1 lb	Beef/pork stewing bones	500g

Instructions:

1. Place all ingredients into a large pot on high heat. Cover and bring to a boil. Reduce heat to low and leave covered 2-4 hours. Chicken broth should come to a caramel colour. Beef broth should be a medium to dark brown.
2. Remove from heat and cool 30 minutes. Strain out bones and discard. Refrigerate overnight.
3. In the morning, fat will have separated and hardened as a top layer. Remove this layer with a spoon and discard (in the garbage, not down your sink).
4. Boil before serving. If storing, ladle cold soup into empty ice cube trays and freeze.

Tip:

- If you've filled all your ice cube trays and still have soup leftover, freeze the remainder in wide-mouthed containers (this way, it will be easier to pop out when you're ready to use it.)
- Once frozen, empty frozen soup cubes into a resealable bag.

VEGETABLE BROTH

Vegetable broth is a great way to use nutritious vegetable parts like stems and ends that you may just be throwing away. Use this broth anytime a recipe calls for chicken, pork or beef broth to help make your recipes vegetarian friendly.

Ingredients:

24oz	Water	3L
1 large	Onion, chopped	1 large
2 large	Carrots, chopped	2 large
2 stems	Celery, chopped	2 stems
3 cloves	Garlic, whole	3 cloves
3	Bay leaves	3
Pinch	Sea salt and pepper	Pinch
	Outer green leaves from one cauliflower	

Instructions:

1. Place all ingredients into a large pot on high heat. Cover and bring to a boil. Reduce heat to low and leave covered 1-2 hours.
2. Remove from heat and cool 30 minutes. Strain out vegetables and bay leaves, and discard. Serve immediately or store for later.

VEGETARIAN OKRA STEW

Prepare this stew as spicy and daring or tame and mild as you want by adjusting the amount of spices. This stew makes a hearty meal alongside rice or millet.

Ingredients:

1 tbsp	Olive oil	15ml
1 large	Onion, chopped	1 large
3-4 cloves	Garlic, halved	3-4 cloves
1	Red bell pepper, diced	1
2	Tomatoes, coarsely chopped	2
2 lbs	Okra, washed, stemmed	1kg
1/2 tsp	Cayenne pepper	2.5ml
1/2 tsp	Paprika	2.5ml
1 tsp	Cumin, ground	5ml
1/2 tsp	Thyme	2.5ml
1/2 tsp	Oregano	2.5ml
1/2 tsp	Rosemary	2.5ml
2 cups	Water	500ml
2 tbsp	Tapioca starch, dissolved	30ml
	Sea salt and pepper to taste	

Instructions:

1. Heat oil in large saucepan over medium heat. Add onion and garlic, stirring 1 minute until they begin to release their aromas.
2. Add remaining vegetables and spices, stirring until tender.
3. Add water and bring to a boil. Reduce heat to simmer uncovered approximately 10-15 minutes, stirring frequently. Okra should be tender enough to pierce with a fork.
4. Dissolve tapioca starch in small amount of cold water. Pour slowly into pot while stirring. Add more if it is still too thin.
5. Serve alone or poured over a hot bed of rice or grain of choice.
6. Freeze cooled leftovers into single or family size portions for a quick meal down the road.

Substitutions:
- Add pinto beans or chickpeas for protein to make this a truly complete meal. Just soak dried beans overnight and boil 20 minutes before adding to step 3.
- You can alternatively use rinsed and drained canned beans.

BUTTERNUT SQUASH SOUP

This is a delicious, hearty and thick soup that makes a great brunch dish on a lazy Sunday afternoon.

Ingredients:

1 medium	Butternut squash	1 medium
3 cups	Water	750ml
2 tbsp	Olive oil	30ml
2 stalks	Celery, diced	2 stalks
1 medium	Onion, sliced thinly	1 medium
1 clove	Garlic, pressed	1 clove

Instructions

1. Rinse squash and carefully peel with a vegetable peeler.
2. Chop into bite sized chunks – the smaller the chunks, the faster it will cook. Remove and discard seeds and pulp.
3. Place into a medium saucepan with water. Bring to a boil, reduce heat to medium-low, cover and let simmer 20-30 minutes, or until squash is very soft. (Alternatively, place the squash and water in a slow cooker on low for 3 hours.)
4. While squash is cooking, pour oil into a separate large frying pan over medium heat. Add garlic and onion, stirring 1 minute until aromas are released.
5. Add celery and 1 tbsp of water to pan. Cover to steam, stirring occasionally, until celery and onions are tender (approximately 2-3 minutes).
6. When squash has finished cooking, pour contents of saucepan, including all water/juices, into a blender. Blend until smooth, adding water if the mixture is too thick.
7. Return squash to saucepan and stir-in other cooked vegetables. Bring back to a boil if desired.
8. Add sea salt and pepper to taste. Serve immediately or refrigerate/freeze to enjoy later.

Substitutions

- Substitute onion with the white section of a leek. You can also chop the green part of a leek and add it in step 6.

FRENCH ONION SOUP

This is a rich and tasty soup. A wonderful start to a romantic dinner for two, or a hardy appetizer for your family and friends. If you plan on making this often, consider investing in a set of French Onion soup bowls with lids.

Ingredients

3 cups	Beef broth (see recipe page 68)	750ml
1 large	Cooking onion	1 large
1/2 cup	Goat cheddar cheese, thinly sliced	125ml
2 slices	Gluten-free bread (optional)	2 slices

Instructions

1. Bring beef broth to a boil in medium sized pot.
2. Slice onions thinly and add to pot.
3. Reduce heat to medium low and simmer covered for 20-30 minutes until onions are very tender and soup develops a strong flavour. Soup may begin to look cloudy.
4. Place goat cheese in the bottom of soup bowls.
5. When ready, pour hot soup over the cheese into bowls.
6. (Optional) Place a slice of bread in each bowl, sitting on top of the soup. Place bowls in oven and broil for 2 minutes. You must use oven-safe bowls for this step!
7. Serve immediately.

Substitutions

- Feel free to experiment with different cheeses.
- If you want to add bread without the fuss, you can also tear smaller pieces of fresh or toasted bread into each bowl just before serving.

TOMATO EGG-DROP SOUP

This is one of my favourite Asian soups. Made with your own chicken broth, you can enjoy this classic dish without the MSG.

Ingredients:

4 cups	Chicken stock (see recipe on page 68)	1L
1 large	Tomato, diced	1 large
2	Eggs, beaten	2

Instructions

1. Place diced tomato in saucepan with chicken stock.
2. Bring to a boil, reduce heat and simmer 2 minutes or until tomato is tender.
3. Whisk eggs in a bowl.
4. Slowly pour a thin stream of eggs into simmering soup while stirring. The eggs should cook quickly into thin and stringy strips.
5. Add sea salt and pepper to taste. Serve immediately.

Winter Melon Watercress Soup

Refreshing and comforting, this is a great soup for any season. Winter melon is considered a "cooling" vegetable in traditional Chinese medicine and believed to help calm inflammation which can cause mouth sores from biting your cheek or lip. Look for winter melon and watercress from your local Chinese grocer. Most fine delis have prosciutto slabs that they will slice fresh. Ask for an end piece which will impart the most flavour to your soup. If you must strictly avoid any gluten contamination, I recommend using broth in place of prosciutto.

Ingredients:

1 small	Winter melon (approx 4-6 cups/1-1.5L)	1 small
1 bunch	Watercress leaves, fresh	1 bunch
5-10	Watercress roots, sliced, fresh or canned	5-10
1	Prosciutto end	1
	OR	
	Pork/beef broth (see recipe on page 68)	

Instructions:

1. Fill a medium saucepan half full with water and add prosciutto. Alternatively, fill saucepan half full with pork or beef broth. Bring to a boil and lower heat to medium low. Simmer 15 minutes if using prosciutto.
2. Cut winter melon in half. Scoop out seeds and pulp with a spoon and discard. Chop into bite sized chunks and discard hard outer skin. Place chopped melon into pot with broth and add more water or broth to cover melon if necessary.
3. If using fresh watercress roots, peel and discard brown outer skin. Canned watercress roots should be rinsed and drained before slicing. Add sliced roots to pot.
4. Gather watercress leaves into a bunch, and chop into 1-2 inch sections. Add to pot with other ingredients.
5. Simmer 10-15 minutes, until winter melon becomes transparent and can be pierced easily by a fork.
6. Add sea salt to taste if desired.
7. Serve immediately, or chill for later.

BREAKFAST

After waking up from a full night of rest, the body starts to ramp up its metabolism to get ready for the day ahead. This is a pivotal point for the body because it's in the first hour of waking that it decides what it needs to do to get through the day. If you skip breakfast, your body can enter a 'starvation mode'. In this state, the body doesn't know when it will get food, and therefore gets ready to store energy instead of burning it. A 2008 study from the Universities of Minnesota and Minneapolis showed that eating breakfast regularly is associated with maintaining a healthy body mass index. So for your optimal health, don't skip this very important meal!

WAFFLES AND PANCAKES 78

HOT CEREAL 79

BLUEBERRY APPLE SMOOTHIE 80

WESTERN SANDWICH 81

ALTERNATIVE YOGURT 82

ALTERNATIVE YOGURT CHEESE 83

QUICK BREAD 84

WAFFLES AND PANCAKES

Ever miss having these treats for breakfast? A delightful weekend breakfast wouldn't be complete without them. Waffles and pancakes use essentially the same recipe, only waffles require slightly more oil to prevent them from sticking to your waffle iron. You can find small electric waffle irons at most stores in the small appliances section.

Ingredients:

2	Eggs	2
3/4 cup	Rice milk	185ml
2 tbsp	Grapeseed oil (4 tbsp/60ml for waffles)	30ml
3/4 cup	Brown rice flour	185ml
1/4 cup	Tapioca starch	65ml
1-1/2 tsp	Baking powder	7.5ml
1/8 tsp	Stevia powder	0.5ml
1/2 tsp	Sea salt	2.5ml

Instructions:
1. Beat eggs until thick. Mix in milk and oil.
2. Add dry ingredients and mix until smooth.
3. Batter should be somewhat thick – easy to pour, but not runny. Adjust thickness as necessary with water or flour.
4. Drop batter into oiled pan over medium heat, or into waffle maker.
5. Serve with butter, maple syrup, agave syrup, fresh fruits, nutmeg and/or cinnamon.

Substitutions:
- Substitute rice milk with any other tolerated milk substitute, or water.
- Substitute brown rice flour with millet flour.
- Serve with coconut oil instead of butter if dairy is not allowed.

HOT CEREAL

Millet replaces oats in this recipe for hot cereal, while nuts and seeds add texture and flavour. To save time, mix dry ingredients together raw and store in a jar for later. When it comes time to cook, all you have to do is pour, rinse, add oil and water then heat.

Ingredients:

1/2 cup	Millet	125ml
1-1/4 cups	Water	315ml
1 tsp	Grapeseed oil	5ml
1/2 cup	Sunflower seeds	125ml
1/4 cup	Flax seeds	65ml
1/4 cup	Slivered almonds	65ml
1/2 tsp	Cinnamon, ground (optional)	2.5ml
	Honey or maple syrup to taste	

Instructions:

1. Rinse millet in a bowl, changing water until it runs clear.
2. Place all ingredients except honey into saucepan. Cover and bring to a boil then reduce heat to low. Simmer 5 minutes covered, stirring occasionally until millet is soft and fluffy. Alternatively, cook cereal in a rice cooker.
3. Scoop into bowls and sweeten with honey or maple syrup.

Substitutions:

- You can use any combination of seeds or nuts. Try pumpkin seeds, sesame seeds, walnuts, pine nuts, pecans or cashews for variety.
- For extra flavour or sweetness, add fresh berries or other fruit just before serving.

BLUEBERRY APPLE SMOOTHIE

This is a simple and nutritious way to start the morning, and is actually what I have for breakfast most days. Try to choose organic fruits, especially if you plan on drinking this often. This recipe is also endless in variations, so feel free to experiment.

Ingredients:

1 cup	Blueberries, fresh or frozen	250ml
2 medium	Apples of your choice, cored, sliced	2 medium
2 tbsp	Almond butter (optional)	30ml
2 tbsp	Honey	30ml
2 tbsp	Goat protein powder	30ml
	Water	

Instructions:
1. Place all ingredients in blender.
2. Add water to cover fruit.
3. Blend 1 minute until smooth and serve.

Substitutions:
- Other protein powders include hemp, brown rice and soy.
- Try these other fruit combinations: strawberries and bananas; nectarines and blueberries; apples and celery; watermelon and pear; or plums, peaches and raspberries.
- For a really healthy green smoothie, try apples with black kale and celery. Replace 1 cup/250ml of water with pineapple juice.
- If you like thicker smoothies, just use less water, add more fruit, or substitute any allowed dairy alternative for water.
- For a cool crunch, add a few ice cubes before blending.
- Substitute stevia, maple syrup or agave syrup for honey.
- To help reduce oxidization (which is what makes cut apples turn brown), try adding pineapple or lemon juice.
- You can also try adding a little spice such as cardamon or cinnamon.

WESTERN SANDWICH

Eggs offer a hearty protein-rich breakfast that will help you get a great start on your day. If you don't have toast, you can enjoy the eggs alone or with a potato hash brown. For healthier bacon, check your local farmer's market for freshly smoked varieties that have no added preservatives, sugar or flavours.

Ingredients:

2 slices	Bacon, chopped	2 slices
1/4 cup	Onion, diced	65ml
3	White mushrooms, diced	3
1/4 cup	Red bell pepper, diced	65ml
3	Eggs, beaten	3
1/4 cup	Goat mozzarella (optional)	65ml
2 slices	Gluten-free toast (optional)	2 slices
	Sea salt and pepper to taste	

Instructions:

1. Heat frying pan over medium heat and add bacon. Cook, stirring, until just done but still soft.
2. Add onions and fry until tender and transparent.
3. Add mushrooms and bell pepper, cook for 1 minute. You may add 1-2 tsp of grapeseed oil if the mixture appears dry.
4. Pour eggs over vegetables, mixing with spatula to scramble.
5. Just as scrambled egg mixture begins to hold its shape, flatten with back of spatula and cook 30 seconds.
6. Flip entire omelette and cook an additional 30 seconds. Sprinkle grated cheese on top. Add sea salt and pepper to taste.
7. Scoop omelette over toast, assemble sandwich and serve.

Tip:

- For a fast breakfast, cook a large batch of veggies and bacon ahead of time, and freeze into single serving sizes.

Substitutions:

- Substitute goat mozzarella with any other permitted cheese.

ALTERNATIVE YOGURT

If you're lucky, you might be able to find goat or sheep yogurt at your local grocery store or farmer's market. If, however, you can't find any or you feel it's too expensive, use this recipe to make your own. All you need is milk of your choice, a candy thermometre (or a clean meat thermometre) and a bacterial starter. The starter can either be from store-bought yogurt, a recent batch of homemade yogurt, or freeze dried bacteria.

Ingredients:

4 cups	Milk (sheep, goat, soy or other)	1L
2 tbsp	Yogurt OR 1 package yogurt starter	60ml

Instructions:

1. Take starter out of refrigerator and place at room temperature to slowly warm up.
2. Heat milk to 185°F (85°C) in a double boiler, stirring occasionally. If you don't have a double boiler, use two pots with one pot that fits inside the other. Water goes into the outer pot, and the milk goes into the inner pot. This will warm the milk more evenly and help prevent scalding.
3. Remove milk from heat and cool to 110°F (43°C), stirring occasionally. For fastest results, immerse the inner pot into a larger pot or bowl filled with cold water. It is important the milk be between 120°F (49°C) and 90°F (32°C) before proceeding.
4. Add the starter and stir gently.
5. Pour mixture into clean glass jars. Cover tightly with a lid.
6. Keep yogurt warm and still to encourage bacteria to incubate and grow for 7 hours (or overnight). Yogurt should be kept close to 100°F (38°C) for the entire incubation period. You can place the jars in an oven with a pilot light on. You can also turn your oven on to bring it to 100°F, then simply leave the oven light on to maintain the temperature (check your oven temperature periodically to be sure it is staying warm enough).
7. Once finished, your yogurt should be custard-like, cheesy in odour, and may have a thin greenish liquid on top. Refrigerate 5-7 hours and serve within 1-2 weeks.
8. Use as a starter within 5-7 days for your next batch.

ALTERNATIVE YOGURT CHEESE

Once you try the previous yogurt recipe, you can take it one step further to make yourself a deliciously creamy and spreadable yogurt cheese. Unlike commercial cheeses, this version has no added sodium. It is very versatile as it will assume the flavour of other ingredients you add to it. Enjoy this cheese as a spread over pancakes, toast, crackers, crumbled over salads, or in other recipes calling for cheese.

Ingredients:

1 batch   Yogurt of your choice   1 batch

Instructions:
1. Pour yogurt onto a large piece of cheesecloth.
2. Carefully and quickly pull up sides of cheesecloth around the yogurt, and tie tightly with a string.
3. Hang the bag by its string inside your refrigerator and place a bowl underneath to catch drippings (called whey). Alternatively, place cheesecloth over a fine sieve suspended over a bowl. Place a small plate and weight (like a soup can) overtop the cloth to help the yogurt drain faster.
4. Leave yogurt to drain for 1-2 days in the refrigerator.
5. Remove cheese from cheesecloth and store tightly in plastic wrap.
6. Reserve the mineral-rich liquid whey for other recipes like pancakes or smoothies.

Variations:
- Yogurt cheese will take on almost any flavour easily.
- For sweet varieties, try adding vanilla, cinnamon, fresh fruit, almond butter or fruit jams.
- For savoury varieties, try mixing with garlic, salt, hot sauce, or herbs like oregano, basil, parsley or dill.

QUICK BREAD

If you're intimidated by the thought of making yeast breads, short on time, or are avoiding yeast, this is a great alternative to try. Unlike yeast breads, which rise before cooking, quick breads rise as they cook in the oven (like cakes).

Ingredients:

1 cup	Brown rice flour	250ml
1/2 cup	Tapioca starch	125ml
2 tsp	Baking powder	10ml
Pinch	Sea salt	Pinch
1/4 cup	Grape seed oil	65ml
1/2 tsp	Stevia powder	2.5ml
1/2 cup	Rice milk	125ml
2	Eggs	2

Instructions:
1. Combine flours, baking powder and salt. In a separate bowl, mix together wet ingredients and stevia.
2. Pour wet ingredients into dry and mix well.
3. Batter should be thick, but still pourable.
4. Spread batter into greased bread pan.
5. Bake 50 minutes at 350°F (175°C).

Substitutions:
- Try substituting rice flour for millet flour.
- Add 1 cup raisins or chopped nuts for a sweet breakfast bread.

GRAINS

With wheat no longer on the menu, there are plenty of other grains available that are nutritious, tasty and easy to prepare. The most convenient way to prepare whole grains is with a rice cooker. As I suggested earlier in the book, look for a rice cooker that has an uncoated stainless steel cooking interior.

Grains will take anywhere from 20-40 minutes to cook, depending on the grain, and how much you're cooking at once. Lighter grains like quinoa will cook much faster than heavier grains like brown rice. Most rice cookers, thankfully, will shut off (or switch to a "keep warm" mode) automatically when your grains have finished cooking. And as an extra bonus, you can buy models with a removable steaming basket. Just place your veggies and/or meats in the basket above your rice as it is cooking and you'll be steaming all your food at once.

STEAMED RICE 86

COCONUT STEAMED RICE 87

SAFFRON STEAMED RICE 88

WILD RICE 89

QUINOA OR MILLET 90

STEAMED RICE

While white jasmine scented rice is very popular, brown rice offers more fibre and nutritional value. Brown rice is slightly nutty in flavour and denser in texture. Because of its higher fibre content, it may also make you feel full longer and help you maintain a more constant energy level.

Ingredients:

2 cups	Brown or white rice	500ml
1 tsp	Oil (optional)	5ml
4 cups	Water OR broth*	1L

For white rice use only 3-1/2 cups (875ml) of water or broth

Instructions (Rice Cooker):
1. Pour rice into rice cooker bowl. Rinse thoroughly and repeatedly, swishing with fingers, until the water runs clear.
2. Drain and add back measured water. You may also add an oil of your choice to help keep rice from sticking to the cooker.
3. Turn on rice cooker. When rice cooker switches off, allow rice to rest for 5 minutes. Fluff with a spatula or spoon before serving.

Instructions (Stovetop):
1. Rinse rice thoroughly and repeatedly, swishing with fingers, until the water runs clear.
2. Coat bottom of pot with oil, and place on stove over high heat. Add rice and water. Stir well.
3. When water comes to a boil, reduce heat to medium-low. Cover partially with lid, allowing some air to escape. Simmer for 15-20 minutes, or until rice has absorbed most or all the liquid.
4. Turn off heat and cover pot tightly with lid. Allow rice to continue steaming another 5-10 minutes. Fluff with a spatula or spoon before serving.

COCONUT STEAMED RICE

This is a popular Thai and Malaysian variation of white rice. This slightly sweet rice is a wonderful side to curries and satays. You can also try it alongside fish or grilled chicken for an extra special dinner, without the extra special effort. For best results, look for a high quality, thick coconut milk (no light varieties). This recipe does not work well with brown rice.

Ingredients:

2 cups	White jasmine rice	500ml
1-1/2 cups	Coconut milk	375ml
2 cups	Water	500ml
1/2 tsp	Salt	2.5ml
2 drops	Stevia liquid	2 drops
1 tsp	Oil (optional)	5ml

Instructions:

1. Pour rice into rice cooker bowl. Rinse thoroughly and repeatedly, swishing with fingers, until the water runs clear.
2. Add all ingredients to rice cooker.
3. Turn on rice cooker. When rice cooker switches off, allow rice to rest for 5 minutes. Fluff with a spatula or spoon before serving.

Instructions (Stovetop):

1. Rinse rice thoroughly and repeatedly, swishing with fingers, until the water runs clear.
2. Coat bottom of pot with oil, and place on stove over high heat. Add remaining ingredients to pot and stir well.
3. When water comes to a boil, reduce heat to medium-low. Cover partially with lid, allowing some air to escape. Simmer for 15-20 minutes, or until rice has absorbed most or all the liquid.
4. Turn off heat and cover pot tightly with lid. Allow rice to continue steaming another 5-10 minutes. Fluff with a spatula or spoon before serving.

Substitutions:

- Substitute 2 drops pure stevia liquid with a pinch of pure stevia powder, or simply omit.

SAFFRON STEAMED RICE

This spiced rice will develop a beautiful bright yellow colour and distinctive flavour. Tumeric is traditionally used in Pakistan as an anti-inflammatory. This is a wonderful spice, but be careful not to spill it on your clothes as it will stain. Enjoy with chicken or fish. This recipe does not work well with brown rice.

Ingredients:

2 cups	White jasmine rice	500ml
1/2 tsp	Saffron threads	2.5ml
1/2 tsp	Tumeric	2.5ml
3-1/2 cups	Water OR broth of choice	875ml
1 tbsp	Fish sauce OR 1/4 tsp sea salt	15ml
1 tsp	Oil (optional)	5ml

Instructions (Rice cooker):
1. Pour rice into rice cooker bowl. Rinse thoroughly and repeatedly, swishing with fingers, until the water runs clear.
2. Add all ingredients to rice cooker.
3. Turn on rice cooker. When rice cooker switches off, allow rice to rest for 5 minutes. Fluff with a spatula or spoon before serving.

Instructions (Stovetop):
1. Rinse rice thoroughly and repeatedly, swishing with fingers, until the water runs clear.
2. Coat bottom of pot with oil, and place on stove over high heat.
3. Add all ingredients to pot, stirring until tumeric is dissolved.
4. When water has come to a boil, reduce heat to medium-low. Cover partially with lid, allowing some air to escape. Simmer for 15-20 minutes, or until rice has absorbed all the liquid.
5. Turn off heat and cover pot tightly with lid. Allow rice to continue steaming another 5-10 minutes. Fluff with a spatula or spoon before serving.

Substitutions:
• If you can't find saffron, you can make this recipe with tumeric only.

WILD RICE

Wild rice is long and black in colour. With a slight crunchiness to it, wild rice is a great way to liven up an otherwise plain side dish. Since it can be quite expensive and overly filling on its own, it is best enjoyed blended with white or brown rice.

Ingredients:

1-1/2 cups	Brown OR white rice	375ml
1/2 cup	Wild rice	125ml
4 cups	Water OR broth of choice	1L
1 tsp	Oil (optional)	5ml

Instructions (Rice Cooker):

1. Pour rice into rice cooker bowl. Rinse rice thoroughly and repeatedly, swishing with fingers, until the water runs clear.
2. Add rice and water to rice cooker. You may also add an oil of your choice to help keep it from sticking to the cooker.
3. Turn on rice cooker. When rice cooker switches off, allow rice to rest for 5 minutes. Fluff with a spatula or spoon before serving.

Instructions (Stovetop):

1. Rinse rice thoroughly and repeatedly, swishing with fingers, until the water runs clear.
2. Coat bottom of pot with oil, and place on stove over high heat. Add rice and water. Stir well.
3. When water comes to a boil, reduce heat to medium-low. Cover partially with lid, allowing some air to escape. Let simmer for 15-20 minutes, or until rice has absorbed most or all the liquid.
4. Turn off heat and cover pot tightly with lid. Allow rice to continue steaming another 5-10 minutes. Fluff with a spatula or spoon before serving.

QUINOA OR MILLET

Quinoa's delicate flavour and aroma makes a great compliment to heavier mains such as pork chops or beef. You can also make it into a tasty salad by adding a few chopped vegetables. If you're pressed for time, this is the fastest grain to cook.

Millet can be cooked in the same way as quinoa. It is slightly heavier in texture than quinoa, but still lighter and fluffier than rice. Millet does not store well, so it's best to cook just enough for one meal.

Both these grains should cook to a light and fluffy texture. If they seem heavy, packed or soggy, continue cooking for another 5 minutes (uncovered if cooked over the stove) to steam off excess water.

Ingredients:

2 cups	Quinoa OR millet	500ml
3-1/2 cups	Water OR broth	875ml
1 tsp	Oil (optional)	5ml

Instructions (Rice Cooker):
1. Rinse grains gently, swishing with fingers, until the water runs clear.
2. Add grains, water and oil to rice cooker.
3. Turn on rice cooker. When cooker switches off, allow grains to rest for 5 minutes before serving.

Instructions (Stovetop):
1. Rinse grains gently, swishing with fingers, until the water runs clear.
2. Coat bottom of pot with 1 tsp oil, and place on stove over high heat. Add grains and water. Stir well.
3. When water comes to a boil, reduce heat to medium-low. Cover partially with lid, allowing some air to escape. Let simmer for 10-15 minutes, or until grains have absorbed most or all the liquid.
4. Turn off heat and cover pot tightly with lid. Allow grains to continue steaming another 5 minutes, or until ready to serve.

VEGETABLES

Vegetables will retain more flavour and nutrients when enjoyed raw, or cooked at lower temperatures with water. That means boiling or steaming. To boil, simply fill a pot 1/4 to 1/2 full with water, add your vegetables and cover. Once the water comes to a boil, reduce the heat to medium-low (or turn heat off completely) and continue cooking covered until tender. Vegetables can also be steamed in a covered pot with a small amount of water, in a steaming basket over a pot of boiling water, or in a steaming basket over a rice cooker. Vegetables continue to cook even after you've removed them from heat, so try to stop cooking your vegetables *just before* they are done.

The easiest way to infuse some natural flavour into your veggies is with garlic, onions, tomato, or spices. For a very characteristic flavour, caramelize your onions and garlic by sautéing them until they turn brown. They will add a wonderfully sweet and flavourful aroma to virtually any dish.

ROASTED ALMOND PECAN SALAD 92

BUTTERED FIDDLEHEADS 94

BROCCOLI 95

ZUCCHINI AND TOMATO 96

SWEET POTATO CHIPS 97

STRING BEANS 98

SNOW PEAS 99

KALE WITH RICE 100

ROASTED FENNEL 101

BOK CHOY WITH MUSHROOMS 102

GUYLAN IN GARLIC 103

BUTTERNUT SQUASH 104

SPAGHETTI SQUASH 105

STUFFED BUTTERCUP SQUASH 106

STUFFED BELL PEPPERS 107

ROASTED ALMOND PECAN SALAD

The roasted nuts in this recipe lend a rich and crunchy texture, and oranges add sweetness and zest. Roasting the nuts is what takes longest in this recipe. So, I recommend cooking enough nuts in one batch to make leftover snacks for later.

Ingredients:

Rosasted nuts

1	Egg white	1
1/2 tsp	Sea salt	2.5ml
1 tsp	Maple syrup	5ml
1 tsp	Rice milk	5ml
2 cups	Pecans	500ml
2 cups	Whole almonds	500ml

Salad

16 oz	Spinach	500g
2	Mandarin oranges, peeled	2
1/4 cups	Balsamic vinegar	65ml
1/4 cups	Olive oil	65ml

Instructions:

1. Before starting, chill a medium mixing bowl and whisk in the refrigerator for 10 minutes.
2. Beat egg white until stiff using chilled electric whisk and bowl. (You can also do this by hand if you don't have the appliance by rubbing a whisk between your palms, as if you were starting a fire. Work quickly or your egg white will fall flat.)
3. Mix in sea salt, maple syrup and rice milk. Add nuts and mix well.
4. Spread over lightly greased/oiled cookie sheet and cook at 325°F (165°C). Stir every 10 minutes until nuts are crispy, approximately 1 hour.
5. While nuts are roasting, rinse and dry spinach. Place in large salad bowl and top with mandarin orange sections.
6. Just before serving, sprinkle roasted nuts over salad. Mix oil and vinegar together and pour over salad. Toss and serve.
7. Keep unused nuts for snacks or appetizers.

Substitutions:

- If you are pressed for time, substitute the roasted nuts for sliced almonds. Simply toast almond slices on a cookie sheet in your oven, or on a tray in your toaster oven for 10 minutes, watching closely so they do not burn.
- Add some zing to the salad by substituting half the spinach with a combination of dandelion leaves, arugula, mustard leaves, endive, or other leafy greens listed in the Vegetables section.

BUTTERED FIDDLEHEADS

Fiddleheads get their name from their resemblance to the head of a fiddle or violin. This wonderful seasonal treat is available in the spring and is packed full of nutrients. Prepare it with the simple recipe below to savour its natural and unique taste.

Ingredients:

1 tbsp	Butter OR olive oil	15ml
1 dozen	Fresh fiddleheads	1 dozen
1 tbsp	Water	15ml
Pinch	Sea salt	Pinch

Instructions:

1. Melt butter in frying pan over medium heat.
2. Rinse fiddleheads and add to pan with water.
3. Cook covered for 2-3 minutes until tender.
4. Sprinkle with sea salt to taste and serve immediately.

BROCCOLI

Choose broccoli that is dark green with no brownish spots on its crown. If there are holes through the bottom of the stems, this is a sign that the vegetable is old and tough.

Ingredients:

1 bunch	Broccoli	1 bunch
	Water	

Instructions:

1. Fill a saucepan with 3 inches of water and heat over stovetop on high.
2. Rinse broccoli, removing stray leaves from stems. Slice through the base of the crown (where the main stem starts to branch off into smaller stems). Cut crown into bite sized sections.
3. Using knife or vegetable peeler, remove tough outer skin on main stem and discard. Slice stem into bite-sized sections.
4. Place broccoli in boiling water, cover and turn heat off. Leave covered approximately 2 minutes.
5. Broccoli is done when a knife or fork can pierce the centre of the stems. Do not overcook!
6. Drain and immerse into cold water. This step will stop the vegetable from cooking any further and help retain its bright green colour.

ZUCCHINI AND TOMATO

This is a great simple dish that can be served as a vegetable side. Keep the juices, and you can also use it as a sauce over rice, pasta or fish. Look for dark green zucchinis, and watch out for fuzzy white mould growing on the tips of stems. Tomatoes should be slightly firm and red. Never refrigerate tomatoes as this damages their flavour.

Ingredients:

2 tbsp	Olive oil	30ml
1 medium	Onion, diced	1 medium
2	Zucchinis, diced	2
1 large	Tomato, diced	1 large
1 tbsp	Water	15ml
	Sea salt and pepper to taste	

Instructions:

1. Heat oil in frying pan over medium heat.
2. Add onion and cook until it begins to brown, stirring occasionally.
3. Add diced zucchinis, tomato and water. Cover and stir occasionally until tender.
4. Add sea salt and pepper to taste.
5. Serve alone as a side dish, or pour over rice, pasta or fish.

SWEET POTATO CHIPS

Sweet potato chips make a great side or afternoon snack. This recipe yields slightly moist "chips", and are best eaten with a fork. Since these are cooked for a longer time in the oven, it is best to use grapeseed oil or another suitable frying oil, as olive oil will smoke.

To save time, slice sweet potatoes with the slicing blade on a food processor or with a mandolin.

Ingredients:

2-3	Sweet potatoes, peeled and thinly sliced	2-3
2 tsp	Grapeseed oil	10ml
1/2 tsp	Garlic powder	2.5ml
1/2 tsp	Paprika	2.5ml
1/2 tsp	Sea salt	2.5ml
1/4 tsp	Ground pepper	1ml

Instructions:

1. Toss all ingredients in a large bowl to combine.
2. Transfer to lightly oiled baking sheet, spreading sweet potatoes evenly in a single layer.
3. Bake at 375°F (190°C) for 25 minutes until edges begin to brown, turning once. Broil for an additional 1-2 minutes. Serve immediately or store in refrigerator.

STRING BEANS

String beans are an easy addition to any meal. Choose beans that are even in colour, firm and full to the touch. Cook enough string beans for a single meal, or make some extra to keep as leftovers for tomorrow's lunch or dinner. Cooked beans can also be frozen to whip up a quick meal at a later date.

Ingredients:

1 bunch	String beans , rinsed, stemmed	1 bunch
	Water	

Instructions:
1. Fill medium saucepan with 2 inches of water and bring to a boil.
2. Gather beans by the handful and cut into bite sized sections. Transfer to pot, cover and reduce heat to medium low.
3. Beans are ready when they appear bright green. They should be slightly tender, but still a little crisp. Do not overcook!

SNOW PEAS

Light and crisp, snow peas are a great accompaniment to a summer meal. Choose peas that are young and firm, but still thin and pliable.

Ingredients:

1 tbsp	Olive oil	15ml
1 clove	Garlic, pressed	1 clove
1 bunch	Snow peas	1 bunch
2 tbsp	Water	30ml

Instructions:
1. Rinse snow peas. Snap off and discard stem ends.
2. Heat oil and garlic in frying pan over medium heat until garlic becomes fragrant, approximately 1 minute.
3. Add snow peas and water.
4. Cook covered for 1 minute and serve.

KALE WITH RICE

This is an easy way to get veggies in your meal. Try cooking rice in large batches and freezing in meal size portions. With pre-cooked frozen rice, this dish (and many others) will only take 5 minutes to prepare.

Ingredients:

2 tbsp	Olive oil	30ml
1 clove	Garlic, pressed	1 clove
1	Onion, diced	1
3 cups	Cooked rice	750ml
2-3	Black or green kale stems, finely chopped	2-3

Instructions:

1. Heat oil and garlic in frying pan over medium heat until garlic becomes fragrant, approximately 1 minute.
2. Add onion and stir until transparent.
3. Add cooked rice to frying pan. If preparing from frozen, add 2tbsp water and cover, stirring occasionally. If rice appears dry, add more water.
4. Once rice is heated, stir in kale and cover for 2-3 minutes.
5. Remove from heat and serve.

Substitutions:

- Make this a complete meal by topping bowls with smoked salmon.
- For added flavour, try adding chopped portobello or oyster mushrooms in step 4.

ROASTED FENNEL

Fennel is a light yet flavourful root vegetable that can compliment almost any other vegetable and meat. Serve this alongside quinoa and fish for a delectable meal.

Ingredients:

1	Fennel bulb	1
3 tbsp	Olive oil	45ml
2 cloves	Garlic, pressed	2 cloves
3 tbsp	Balsamic vinegar	45ml

Instructions:

1. Rinse fennel root thoroughly. Slice through centre vertically. Place cut side down and slice thinly in vertical strips. The fennel will resemble sliced onions. If your root has any loose leaves, remove and reserve for later.
2. Spread fennel evenly over a baking sheet.
3. In a small bowl, mix together oil, garlic and vinegar. Drizzle over fennel slices.
4. Cook in oven at 350°F (175°C) for 15-20 minutes, or until vegetable is cooked through and beginning to brown.
5. Sprinkle with reserved leaves and serve.

Substitutions:

- Sprinkle with poppy seeds or chia seeds before baking for added texture.

BOK CHOY WITH MUSHROOMS

This delicately flavoured vegetable is a great addition to noodle or rice dishes. It makes an excellent accompaniment with its mild and sweet taste.

Bok choy tends to have quite a bit of dirt and small stones hidden between its leaves. If preparing baby bok choy bunches whole, soak the vegetables in a large bowl of water or in your sink for several minutes to allow dirt to settle out. Alternatively, you can break off leaves at their base in order to rinse them individually.

Ingredients:

5	Baby bok choy bunches, rinsed	5
1 tsp	Grapeseed oil	5ml
1 clove	Garlic, pressed	1 clove
1/4 cup	Pine mushrooms	65ml
1 tbsp	Wheat-free tamari sauce	15ml
1/2 cup	Water	125ml

Instructions:

1. Heat oil in saucepan over medium heat. Add garlic, stirring until aromatic, approximately 1 minute.
2. Add remaining ingredients and cover pot. Reduce heat to low and cook approximately 1-2 minutes, or until bok choy is as tender as desired.

Substitutions:

- Substitute 5 bunches baby bok choy with 5 stems of full sized bok choy. Separate each leaf from the base, rinse well, and slice horizontally into bite sized sections.
- Substitute pine mushrooms for dried shitake mushrooms. Dried mushrooms should be pre-soaked 1 hour, rinsed and sliced thinly.
- To prepare as a very simple side dish, bok choy may also be prepared alone, or with garlic only.

GAILAN IN GARLIC

Gailan is a stronger flavoured vegetable with a hearty texture, slightly bitter and slightly sweet taste. It is most often served with oyster sauce in Chinese cuisine, but unfortunately oyster sauce often contains gluten, sugar and MSG.

Gailan is a good substitute in recipes calling for broccoli, but with its distinctive flavour, can easily be served on its own or with milder flavoured foods like tofu.

Ingredients:

1 tbsp	Sesame seed oil	15ml
2 cloves	Garlic, pressed	2 cloves
1 bunch	Gailan	1 bunch
1/4 cup	Water	65ml

Instructions:

1. Heat oil in saucepan over medium heat. Add garlic, stirring until aromatic, approximately 1 minute.
2. Separate individual gailan stems and rinse thoroughly. Cut stems into 2 inch sections.
3. Add gailan and water to saucepan and cover. Cook 2-3 minutes, or until stems can be easily pierced by a fork.

Substitutions:

- While the strong aroma of sesame oil compliments guylan, you can also substitute for a lighter flavoured oil such as grapeseed.
- Sauté tofu or thinly sliced beef between step 1 and step 2 to make this a complete protein rich dish.

BUTTERNUT SQUASH

This light and slightly sweet squash makes a lovely side in place of mashed potatoes. It also makes great baby food.

Ingredients:

1	Butternut squash	1
1 cup	Water	250ml

Instructions:

1. Rinse and peel butternut squash with vegetable peeler. Be very careful when peeling or cutting because peeled squash is very slippery.
2. Chop into small cubes. The smaller the cubes, the faster it will cook. Remove and discard seeds and pulp.
3. Place chopped squash and water into slow cooker. Cook on low for 3 hours or until very tender. OR Place chopped squash in steaming basket and steam for 30-40 minutes or until very tender.
4. Remove squash, drain and reserve liquid for another recipe if desired. Mash with a fork or potato masher. To make a very smooth mixture for soups or baby food, use a blender to puree squash and cooking liquid.
5. Serve alone, with sea salt, butter and/or maple syrup.

SPAGHETTI SQUASH

This is a fun squash to cook for kids and sometimes shows up as a whole food substitute for pasta. Once cooked, the squash can be scraped out in long tubes, just like spaghetti!

Ingredients:

1	Spaghetti squash	1
1 tsp	Grapeseed oil	5ml
	Sea salt to taste	

Instructions:

1. Rinse squash and cut in half lengthwise. Drizzle cut ends with oil.
2. Place cut sides down on a baking sheet. Cook in oven at 350°F (175°C) for 30-45 minutes, or until squash can be pierced with a fork.
3. Gently scrape inside of squash with a spoon to remove layer by layer of "spaghetti". Serve with sea salt and/or butter.

STUFFED BUTTERCUP SQUASH

This is a very easy dish to prepare, and an impressive item to serve at the dinner table. And since the squash is the bowl, you'll have one less dish to wash.

Ingredients:

1	Buttercup squash	1
2 tbsp	Butter	30ml
2 tbsp	Maple syrup	30ml
1-1/2 cups	Chopped pecans, cashews, almonds and/or walnuts	375ml

Instructions:

1. Wash buttercup squash. Cut a circular opening around the stem and discard seeds and pulp, just like you would a pumpkin. Take the "cap" that you just cut out, and slice away a small section from one side. When you close the squash, this will leave a small gap to allow air to escape.
2. Stuff squash with nuts, followed by butter and maple syrup. Close the squash with its cap and place on cookie sheet.
3. Cook at 350°F (175°C) for 30-40 minutes, until inside of squash can be easily pierced by a fork.
4. Serve on a plate with a large spoon. Each person can scoop out their own portion directly from the squash.

Substitutions:

- For a dairy-free version, substitute butter with grapeseed oil or coconut oil.
- Substitute maple syrup with honey.

Stuffed Bell Peppers

This is a deceivingly impressive looking dish that is very easy to prepare. According to the Environmental Working Group in the U.S., sweet bell peppers have among the highest pesticide loads of all commonly eaten fruits and vegetables. So, be sure chose certified organic varieties when available.

Ingredients:

2	Bell peppers, colours of choice	2
1/4 cup	Black or green olives	65ml
1 small	Tomato, seeded and diced	1 small
1/2 cup	Crumbled goat feta	125ml
2 tbsp	Olive oil	30ml
	Sea salt and pepper to taste	

Instructions:

1. Slice bell peppers in half through stems. Remove and discard seeds. Place peppers on cookie sheet, open ends facing up.
2. Distribute remaining ingredients evenly inside pepper halves.
3. Bake at 350°F (175°C) for 20 minutes until skin begins to darken.

WRAPS AND SANDWICHES

By simply using gluten-free wraps and gluten-free breads, you can still enjoy these convenient portable lunches. Your cheapest option will be to use dried rice wraps, which can be stored for a very long time and are very easy to use. Look for these at your local Asian grocer or in the ethnic food section at your regular supermarket.

CHICKEN HUMMUS SALAD ROLLS 110

VIETNAMESE SPRING ROLLS 111

CHICKEN SANDWICH...112

EGG OR TUNA SALAD SANDWICH 114

Chicken Hummus Salad Rolls

With hummus and goat cheese, this hearty roll can easily be made into a vegetarian meal with the omission of chicken.

Ingredients:

5	Dried rice wraps	5
1 lb	Chicken breast strips, cooked	500g
1/2 cup	Hummus	125ml
1/2 cup	Goat cheese, grated	125ml
1/2 cup	Carrots, raw shredded	125ml
2 leaves	Romaine lettuce, shredded	2 leaves

Instructions:

1. Rinse and prepare vegetables. Set aside.
2. Fill a pie plate, or other large dish, with warm water. Holding one dried rice wrap in both hands, dip half the wrap into warm water and slowly rotate. Continue rotating the wrap until it is completely soft. (Keeping half of the wrap in water, and the other half out of the water in your hands will keep it from folding on itself and sticking together.) Place wrap carefully on a plate.
3. Distribute remaining ingredients in a horizontal strip along the bottom third of the wrap.
4. Pick up edge closest to you and fold wrap snugly around filling. Fold both sides in towards the centre, and continue rolling the wrap away from you to close. Repeat with each wrap.
5. Wraps can be covered and refrigerated for later.

Substitutions:

- Substitute chicken with roasted duck, beef, pork, turkey or shrimp. Pâté and cheese are great ways to add different flavours.
- Add cooked vermicelli (rice noodles) for additional filling.
- Add sliced bell peppers (green, yellow, orange or red) to add colour.
- For a really quick wrap, put everything in a large romaine lettuce leaf in place of rice wraps.

VIETNAMESE SPRING ROLLS

Most often served in Vietnamese cuisine, these spring rolls are sometimes called cold spring rolls, or Vietnamese salad rolls. In many restaurants, you may also find them deep fried. While these rolls won't be as big as traditional wheat wraps, they are just as versatile.

Ingredients:

5	Dried rice wraps	5
1 lb	Chicken strips	500g
	OR shrimp OR pork (cooked)	
4 oz	Vermicelli	120g
8 oz	Bean sprouts	225g
1/2 cup	Carrots, raw shredded	125ml
2 leaves	Romaine lettuce, shredded	2 leaves
5 leaves	Fresh basil and/or Cilantro (optional)	5 leaves
1	Sweet bell pepper, sliced thinly	1
	Warm water	

Instructions:

1. Rinse and prepare vegetables. Set aside. Boil and drain vermicelli and set aside.
2. Fill a pie plate, or other large dish, with warm water. Holding one dried rice wrap in both hands, dip half the wrap into warm water and slowly rotate. Continue rotating the wrap until it is completely soft. (Keeping half of the wrap in water, and the other half out of the water in your hands will keep it from folding on itself and sticking together.) Place wrap carefully on a plate.
3. Distribute remaining ingredients in a horizontal strip along the bottom third of the wrap.
4. Pick up edge closest to you and fold wrap snugly around filling. Fold both sides in towards the centre, and continue rolling the wrap away from you to close.
5. Repeat with each wrap.
6. Serve with fish sauce to dip. Wraps can be covered and refrigerated for later.

CHICKEN SANDWICH

Processed meats often contain gluten, dairy, sulphites and other not-so-friendly food allergens. So instead, use whole meats to make healthy and tasty sandwiches for easy school and work lunches. To save time, cook several chicken breasts and make a week's worth of sandwiches so that they're ready to go each morning. To prevent bread from going soggy, either dry salad greens thoroughly, or pack separately and finish assembling your sandwiches just before eating.

Ingredients:

1 small	Chicken breast	1 small
1 stem	Thyme, fresh (or 1/2 tsp dried)	1 stem
1 tbsp	Grapeseed oil	15ml
Pinch	Sea salt and pepper	Pinch
2 slices	Gluten-free bread	2 slices
1 leaf	Lettuce	1 leaf
	Condiments of your choice	

Instructions:

1. Place chicken breast in shallow dish and rub with thyme, oil, salt and pepper. For most flavourful results, cover and marinate in re-frigerator 2 hours or overnight (optional).
2. Place chicken on cookie sheet or grilling pan in oven at 350°F (175°C) for 10 minutes, or until internal temperature reaches 165°F (74°C) and meat is white throughout. Do not overcook – this will result in dry, tough meat.
3. While chicken is cooking, rinse and dry lettuce.
4. Remove chicken and allow to rest 5 minutes before slicing into thin strips.
5. Toast bread and assemble sandwiches as desired.
6. Wrap in wax or parchment paper and secure with elastic or tape. Or pack in reusable containers for a waste-free lunch.

Substitutions:

- You can make endless varieties of sandwiches. Try adding fresh tomatoes, crumbled bacon (that you cook yourself, not freeze dried bacon bits), cucumbers, pickles, red onions, hot peppers or cheese.

- Use any freshly cooked and sliced meat of your choice: dark chicken meat, turkey, pork, peameal bacon or roast beef.

- Cook the chicken to your liking with a variety of herbs like oregano, basil, coriander, cayenne, paprika, garlic or ginger. For variety throughout the week, you can even cook each chicken breast differently.

EGG OR TUNA SALAD SANDWICH

Here's a quick and easy sandwich that can be vegetarian friendly. To prevent bread from going soggy, pack individual servings of egg-salad separately from bread, and assemble the sandwich when you're ready to eat it.

Depending on the type of stove and pot you are using, cooking times may vary for your eggs. Your eggs are done when the yoke is brightly coloured and slightly jelly-like in consistency. If your yokes are hard, powdery, and green around the edges, they are overcooked.

Ingredients:

3	Eggs	3
	OR	
1 can	Tuna	1 can
1 stem	Celery, finely diced	1 stem
1/4 cup	Peas, fresh or frozen	65 ml
2-3 tbsp	Mayonnaise	30-45ml
2 slices	Gluten-free bread	2 slices
	Condiments of your choice	
	Sea salt and pepper to taste	

Instructions:
1. Bring small pot of water to a boil. Gently spoon eggs into water. Boil uncovered 3-4 minutes. Remove and submerge into cold water 1 minute. Peel away and discard shells. (Skip this step if using tuna.)
2. Cut eggs into small cubes. If using tuna, rinse, drain and separate meat into chunks with a fork.
3. Combine egg or tuna in bowl with diced celery, peas, mayonnaise, salt and pepper.
4. Mixture should stick together easily. Add more mayonnaise if desired.
5. Toast bread and assemble sandwich.
6. Wrap in wax or parchment paper and secure with elastic or tape.

Substitutions:
- Enjoy as a side dish without the bread, or as an hors d'oeuvre scooped on top of crackers.

ENTRÉES

The following entrees include many of my personal favourites that may at first seem off-limits. With just a few simple changes, you'll be able to enjoy familiar dishes like pizza, hamburgers and crab crakes.

CHICKEN FRIED RICE..116

CHICKEN WITH CASHEWS 117

WHOLE ROAST CHICKEN WITH ROOT VEGETABLES 118

CHILI 120

VENISON STEW 122

HAMBURGERS 124

ROAST BEEF...125

HONEY-GARLIC BBQ RIBS 126

BREADED PORK CHOPS..127

PORTOBELLO MUSHROOMS WITH PORSCHIUTTO 128

POACHED BLACK COD 129

GARLIC BUTTER SALMON..130

BUTTERED LOBSTER OR CRAB 131

SEAFOOD GUMBO 132

CRAB CAKES 134

GARLIC SHRIMP 135

HERBED PIZZA CRUST..136

PORSCIUTTO GOAT CHEESE PIZZA 137

ROASTED TOMATO PASTA SAUCE..138

GREEN PESTO 139

LASAGNE...140

RISOTTO 142

QUICHE..143

TOFU HOTPOT 144

CHICKEN FRIED RICE

I used to make this quite often when I was a student. This is a great way to use up leftover rice or leftover chicken, and is an easy to prepare single-dish meal.

Ingredients:

1 tsp	Grapeseed oil	15ml
2	Eggs, beaten	2
1 clove	Garlic, pressed	1 clove
2 stems	Green onion, finely sliced	2 stems
1/2 cup	Green peas, frozen or fresh	125ml
2 cups	Brown rice, cooked	500ml
1	Chicken breast, cooked, diced	1
1 tbsp	Wheat-free tamari sauce	15ml
2 stems	Cilantro, fresh (optional)	2 stems

Instructions:

1. Heat oil in saucepan over medium heat. Add eggs and scramble until slightly runny. Scoop into a bowl and set aside.
2. Add garlic to saucepan, stirring until aroma is released, approximately 1 minute. Add more oil if saucepan is dry.
3. Stir in onion and continue cooking 1 minute until aroma is released.
4. Stir in rice and cook covered 2 minutes until heated through, stirring occasionally. If rice appears very dry, add 1 tbsp (15ml) water and cover.
5. Add chicken and tamari. Continue cooking 1 minute, covered. (If rice is too moist, cook uncovered.)
6. Add back reserved eggs and mix well with rice.
7. Scoop onto plates and top with torn cilantro leaves (optional).

Substitutions

- For a vegetarian version, substitute chicken with 1/2 a block of firm tofu.
- Substitute chicken with pork, beef, fish or other leftover meat.
- Substitute green onion with yellow or white onion.
- Substitute garlic with shallots for a slightly different aroma.

CHICKEN WITH CASHEWS

The cashews in this recipe lend a pleasant crunchy texture to this dish, while bell peppers add a hint of sweetness. This is a great dish with rice, and is even better with coconut steamed rice. When possible, choose certified organic bell peppers.

Ingredients:

2	Chicken breasts	2
2 tbsp	Wheat-free tamari sauce	30ml
1 tsp	Sesame seed oil	5ml
1 tsp	Grapeseed oil	5ml
2 cloves	Garlic, minced	2 cloves
1 small	Onion, roughly chopped	1 small
2 stems	Green onion, finely sliced	2 stems
1	Red bell pepper, chopped	1
1	Green bell pepper, chopped	1
1/2 cup	Cashew nuts	125ml

Instructions:

1. Slice chicken breasts into thin, bite-sized slices. Place in medium bowl and mix with tamari and sesame seed oil.
2. Heat oil in large frying pan or saucepan. Add garlic and cook 1 minute until it releases its aroma.
3. Add chicken and cook 2 minutes, covered, stirring occasionally until chicken is cooked through. Remove chicken and reserve for later.
4. In the same pan, add grapeseed oil and both kinds of onions. Cook covered 1 minute until softened.
5. Cut bell peppers in half through stems. Remove and discard seeds and stems and chop into bite sized chunks. Add to pan and cook, covered 1 minute until softened.
6. Add cashews and cooked chicken, stirring 1 minute to combine flavours. Transfer to plate and serve.

WHOLE ROAST CHICKEN WITH ROOT VEGETABLES

Here's a great way to cook a chicken with roasted vegetables to help make a nicely rounded meal. And when you're done cooking, keep the bones to make chicken stock for later.

Ingredients:

2 large	Sweet potatoes, peeled, cubed	2 large
2 large	Carrots, peeled, chopped	2 large
3	Parsnips, peeled	3
1 dozen	Radishes, peeled	1 dozen
1 small	Onion, diced	1 small
2 tbsp	Olive oil	30ml
3 tbsp	Butter, room temperature OR olive oil	45ml
2 tbsp	Sage, finely chopped	30ml
2 cloves	Garlic, pressed	2 cloves
1 whole	Chicken	1 whole
8 oz	Tatsoi leaves	250g
8 oz	Mustard leaves	250g
1/4 cup	Water	65ml
1 tbsp	Tapioca starch	15ml
1/2 cup	White wine (optional)	125ml

Instructions:

1. Coat root vegetables and onion with olive oil and place in roasting pan.
2. Mix butter, sage and garlic in small bowl. Rub 1 tbsp of spiced butter over chicken skin. Dot remaining butter over root vegetables.
3. Place chicken on top of vegetables in roasting pan. Roast in oven at 375°F (190°C) for approximately 60 minutes, or until internal temperature reaches 180°F (82°C) and vegetables are tender.
4. Spread tatsoi and mustard leaves over large serving platter.
5. Remove chicken from oven when done and allow to rest for 5 minutes. Scoop cooked root vegetables overtop of greens. Transfer chicken to cutting board, allowing juices to drain into roasting pan.

6. Carve chicken and place meat onto serving plate over vegetables.
7. Dissolve tapioca starch in water and pour into roasting pan with wine.
8. Place roasting pan on stovetop over medium-high heat and bring to a boil. Reduce heat and simmer for 2 minutes, stirring frequently. Add sea salt and pepper to taste. Transfer to bowl or gravy boat and serve with chicken.

Substitutions:
- Substitute whole chicken with chicken breast or thighs, and reduce cooking time to 20-30 minutes.
- Substitute sage with thyme or oregano.
- Add 1 cup whole cranberries (fresh or frozen) and 10 drops stevia liquid to roasting pan and cook with root vegetables for a festive touch.
- Substitute tatsoi and mustard leaves for other tender leafy greens like spinach, arugula or endive.

Tip:
- For a moister chicken breast, place chicken in roasting pan breast side down.

CHILI

Here is a very tasty gluten-free recipe for this wonderfully familiar favourite. There are endless possibilities to customize the spice mix, so feel free to experiment!

Ingredients:

1 cup	Dried white kidney beans	250ml
1 cup	Dried red kidney beans	250ml
1 cup	Dried chickpeas	250ml
4 tbsp	Olive oil	60ml
2	Portobello mushrooms, diced	2
1 lb	Ground turkey	500g
2	Onions, diced	2
3	Carrots, peeled and diced	3
4 stalks	Celery, diced	4 stalks
2	Jalapeno peppers, chopped	2
2	Large tomatoes, diced	2
3 cups	Chicken broth	750ml
1 tsp	Paprika	5ml
1 tbsp	Oregano	15ml
2 tbsp	Chilli powder	30ml
3 tbsp	Tapioca starch	45ml
1 tsp	Sea salt	5ml
1 tsp	Black peppercorns	5ml

Instructions:
1. In large bowl, soak white kidney beans, red kidney beans and chickpeas in water overnight.
2. In large frying pan, heat 2 tbsp oil over medium heat. Add mushrooms and cook until tender. Transfer to slow cooker.
3. Add 2 tbsp oil to same pan over medium heat. Add ground turkey, stirring until browned. Transfer to slow cooker, leaving liquids in pan.
4. Add onions, carrots, celery and jalapeno peppers to same pan and cook until softened. Transfer to slow cooker.

5. Add tomatoes, broth and spices to same frying pan and bring to a boil. Transfer to slow cooker.
6. Transfer beans and chickpeas to slow cooker and stir.
7. Cover and cook on low for 8 to 10 hours, or on high for 4 to 5 hours.
8. Just before serving, turn slow cooker to high. Dissolve tapioca starch with a small amount of cold water. Add to slow cooker and stir. Cover and allow to thicken 10 minutes.

Substitutions:
- For a vegetarian version, substitute turkey with 2-4 additional portobello mushrooms, and substitute chicken broth with vegetable broth. The portobello mushrooms give this recipe a meaty flavour and texture.
- Substitute turkey with beef, pork or chicken. You can use ground meats or stewing meats.
- Substitute dried beans/chickpeas with canned versions. Be sure to rinse and drain before using.
- For a thicker chili, blend 1-2 cups cooked beans/chickpeas in a food processor or blender. Add back to remaining chili and stir well.

VENISON STEW

This is a great, hearty stew that can be enjoyed over a bed of grains like rice, quinoa or millet. Set it in your slow cooker in the morning, and come home to a hot stew for dinner. Freeze leftovers in single or family sized servings for a quick meal when you're pinched for time.

Ingredients:

1.5 lbs	Stewing venison, cubed	750g
2 tbsp	Olive oil	30ml
2 medium	Onions, cubed	2 medium
4 stalks	Celery, chopped	4 stalks
2 large	Carrots, peeled, chopped	2 large
2 medium	Potatoes, cubed	2 medium
2 medium	Sweet potatoes, peeled, cubed	2 medium
1 large	Tomato, cubed	1 large
2 tsp	Mustard powder	10ml
1	Bay leaf	1
1 tbsp	Rosemary	15ml
1 tsp	Sea salt	5ml
1 tsp	Black peppercorns	5ml
1-1/2 cups	Water, boiling	375ml
2 tbsp	Tapioca starch	30ml

Instructions:

1. Heat olive oil over medium heat in large frying pan.
2. Brown venison 2 minutes per side and transfer to slow cooker, reserving as much oil as you can in frying pan.
3. Add prepared vegetables to frying pan and cook until slightly tender. Transfer to slow cooker.
4. Add remaining ingredients. Cook on low for 7-9 hours.
5. When finished cooking, turn slow cooker up to high. Dissolve tapioca starch in small amount of cold water and mix into stew. Cook covered for 10 minutes until thickened. Add additional starch if desired.

Substitutions:
- Substitute venison with beef or pork.
- Add chopped jalapeño pepper for a spicy version.
- If you're missing any vegetable, simply substitute it with any of the remaining vegetables. I don't recommend omitting potatoes or carrots, as these help make the venison flavour more mild and palatable.
- Substitute celery with fennel bulb for a richer flavour.

HAMBURGERS

Store bought hamburgers are often filled with gluten, soy and sugar. Luckily, this is also another very easy item to make. Hamburgers can be as simple or elaborate as you want them to be. You can make them out of straight ground meat, or add some spices and extra binders to make them smoother and tastier. You can form patties very easily by hand, but if you plan on making a lot of hamburgers, you can buy a hamburger press for even patties every time.

Ingredients:

2 lb	Beef, ground	1kg
1/2	Onion, finely chopped	1/2
1	Egg, beaten	1
1/2 cup	Rice flakes	125ml
1 tbsp	Tapioca starch	15ml
1/2 tsp each	Coriander, paprika, sea salt, pepper	2.5ml each
1 tsp	Garlic powder	5ml

Instructions:
1. Combine all ingredients in a large bowl and mix well.
2. Measure 1/2 cup of meat mixture and press between your palms to make a round patty. Try to ensure thickness is even throughout. Repeat until all meat is used. If storing and freezing for later, separate patties with a piece of wax paper.
3. Place on hot barbeque grill for 3-5 minutes per side, until cooked completely through. Alternatively, cook in oven at 350°F (175°C) on a grilling pan for 5-10 minutes per side. Meat should be well done and cooked throughout with no pink centres.
4. Serve with gluten-free buns, or wrapped in large romaine lettuce leaves with condiments of choice.

Substitutions:
- Substitute beef and coriander with pork and coriander, or chicken and oregano.
- Substitute rice flakes with quinoa flakes, leftover rice, gluten-free bread crumbs, 2 tbsp (30ml) psyllium husks or tapioca starch.
- Top with bacon, grilled mushrooms and/or cheese.

ROAST BEEF

Beef will retain its juices best if the outside is first seared before roasting in the oven. Keep leftover roast beef slices for tasty lunch sandwiches or wraps.

Ingredients:

1 medium	Roasting beef	1 medium
2 tbsp	Grapeseed oil	30ml
3 cloves	Garlic, pressed	3 cloves
2 tsp	Paprika	10ml
1 tsp	Rosemary	5ml
1 tsp	Sea salt	5ml
1/4 tsp	Cayenne pepper	1ml
1/2 tsp	Ground pepper	2.5ml

Instructions:

1. Rub all sides of roast with oil and spices. Place in refrigerator to marinate 30 minutes or overnight.
2. Heat large frying pan over high heat with 1 tbsp (15ml) oil. Transfer roast into pan, browning each side approximately 2 minutes.
3. Transfer onto roasting pan and cook in oven at 350°F (175°C) approximately 40-60 minutes, or until internal temperature reaches 140°F (60°C - rare), 160°F (70°C - medium) or 170°F (75°C - well done).
4. Remove from oven and allow roast to rest 5 minutes before slicing.
5. Serve immediately with rice, pasta, millet or quinoa.

Substitutions:

- If you have an oven-proof cast iron skillet, you can use it in step 2 to brown the meat, and simply transfer the entire skillet into the oven for step 3. See the Equipment section in Chapter 2 for important notes about cooking in cast iron.
- Substitute basil with rosemary. You can also substitute all the spices with garlic, ginger and wheat-free tamari.

HONEY-GARLIC BBQ RIBS

Here's a hearty and meaty favourite sure to please the meat lover. Unlike store bought "honey-garlic flavoured" ribs that often don't even contain honey, these ribs get their true flavour from real honey and fresh garlic.

Ingredients :

1 rack	Pork ribs	1 rack
1/2 cup	Honey	125ml
1/4 cup	Wheat-free tamari	65ml
1/4 cup	Vinegar	65ml
2 cloves	Garlic, pressed	2 cloves
1 tsp	Garlic powder	5ml
1/2 tsp	Sea salt	2.5ml
1 tsp	Baking soda	5ml

Instructions:

1. Combine all ingredients, except pork ribs, in a small mixing bowl.
2. Place ribs on grilling pan. Brush sauce onto both sides. Pour excess sauce over ribs, meat side up.
3. Bake at 375°F (190°C) for one hour, turning every 20 minutes.
4. Serve immediately with vegetables and rice or other grain of choice.

BREADED PORK CHOPS

This is a great way to use up all those crumbs from your gluten-free crackers and breads that might otherwise go to waste. If you don't have any crumbs around, you can crush your own or simply use flours (see substitutions below).

Ingredients:

4	Pork chops	4
1	Egg, beaten	1
2 tbsp	Soy milk or milk substitute	30ml
1 cup	Gluten-free cracker crumbs	100g
1/2 tsp	Oregano	2.5ml
1/2 tsp	Garlic powder	2.5ml
1 tbsp	Paprika	15ml
2 tbsp	Chili powder	30ml
Pinch	Sea salt and pepper	Pinch

Instructions:

1. In small bowl, beat eggs with soy milk.
2. Place crackers in a clean plastic bag, wrap in a dish towel and crush by rolling with a rolling pin. Crumbs should be medium to fine. Pour into medium sized bowl or flat baking dish, and mix in spices.
3. Coat pork chops in flour mixture. Follow by coating with egg mixture, then flour mixture again.
4. Spread pork chops in a single layer on a baking sheet. Bake in oven at 350°F (175°C) for approximately 30-40 minutes, turning once.

Substitutions:

- If you can tolerate cheese, try adding 1/4 cup (65ml) of grated parmesan cheese or other strong flavoured goat cheese for extra flavour.
- If you don't have gluten-free crackers, substitute with 1/2 cup (125ml) millet flour and 1/2 cup (125ml) tapioca starch.

PORTOBELLO MUSHROOMS WITH PROSCIUTTO

Here's a quick and easy recipe for a light lunch or accompaniment to dinner. If you're missing either the mushrooms or prosciutto, the recipe will still work just fine.

Ingredients:

1 tsp	Olive oil	5ml
1/2	Small onion, sliced thinly	1/2
2	Portobello mushrooms	2
5 slices	Prosciutto	5 slices
Pinch	Sea salt	Pinch

Instructions:

1. Heat oil in large frying pan over medium heat.
2. Spread onion slices evenly in pan and cook until transparent.
3. As onions are cooking, prepare mushrooms by removing and discarding stems. Slice mushroom caps thinly and add to frying pan. Stir to coat with oil and cook covered 1 minute.
4. Spread prosciutto slices evenly on a large serving plate. Pour hot mushrooms and onions overtop prosciutto. If you prefer cold prosciutto, place meat along plate edges instead.
5. Sprinkle with sea salt and serve immediately.

POACHED BLACK COD WITH
RICE NOODLES AND BOK CHOY

Black cod is a moist and buttery fish, mild in flavour and smooth in texture. The secret to cooking great fish is to remove it from the heat right when it's done, so that it doesn't overcook. Fish is ready when the flesh flakes off with gentle pressure from a fork.

Ingredients:

1 fillet	Black cod	1 fillet
1 tsp	Ginger, fresh or ground	5ml
1 stem	Green onion, sliced	1 stem
1 bunch	Dry rice noodles	1 bunch
3-5	Baby bok choy bunches, rinsed, sliced	3-5
1 tbsp	Wheat-free tamari sauce	15ml
1 tbsp	Fish sauce	15ml
1 tbsp	Sesame oil	15ml

Instructions:
1. Prepare cod by removing bones with a tweezer. While this step is optional, it does make eating it easier and more enjoyable.
2. Where cod is thicker than 1 inch, slice horizontally through half the thickness. This will help the fish cook quickly and evenly.
3. Fill pot with 2 inches of water, and add ginger and green onion. Bring to a boil. Reduce heat to medium and add fish, skin side down. Simmer covered 7 minutes.
4. Remove fish from pot with slotted spoon, and set aside.
5. Add rice noodles and bok choy to saucepan with leftover hot water. Cover and cook 1 minute until noodles and vegetables are tender. Drain and add to fish.
6. Pour tamari sauce, fish sauce and sesame oil over fish and noodles. Toss noodles and serve immediately.

Substitutions:
- Substitute rice noodles with gluten-free pasta of your choice.
- Substitute baby bok choy with 3-5 full sized stems.
- Substitute bok choy with broccoli, string beans, snow peas or bean sprouts.

GARLIC BUTTER SALMON

For some reason, salmon always tastes better to me when it's grilled on a barbeque. Be sure to keep a close eye on the fish so that it doesn't overcook.

Ingredients:

1	Salmon steak or fillet	1
2 cloves	Garlic, pressed	2 cloves
1 small	Onion, sliced thinly	1 small
2 tbsp	Butter OR olive oil	30ml
1/2 tsp	Sea salt	2.5ml
	Ground pepper to taste	

Instructions:

1. Cut out a sheet of parchment paper 3 times the size of the fish.
2. Spread onion slices in centre of paper, topped with salmon.
3. Rub garlic over salmon, add butter and salt.
4. Fold paper to wrap fish. Over-wrap with aluminium foil, shiny side in. (You can skip the parchment paper, but I prefer to use it so that the fish doesn't come into direct contact with the aluminium. Never place parchment paper directly on your grill.)
5. Place wrapped fish on barbeque grill at 400°F (205°C). Cook approximately 10 minutes, or until flesh can flake easily with a fork.
6. Add freshly ground pepper to taste. Serve with rice or pasta.

BUTTERED LOBSTER OR CRAB

Look for small lobsters, not much larger than the size of your hand – these ones tend to be very tasty. To really enjoy lobster (or crab), invest in one or two butter melting dishes. These inexpensive dishes usually have a small mounted bowl overtop a tea light candle that will keep your butter melted at the table. Small lobster forks and shell crackers are also a good idea to keep in your drawer for these special occasions.

Ingredients:

1	Small lobster	1
	OR	
6	Crab legs	6
2 tbsp	Butter OR spiced oil	30ml

Instructions:

1. Fill the bottom of a steamer with 2 inches of water and insert steaming basket. Cover and bring to a boil over high heat.
2. Once water is boiling, place whole lobster (or crab legs) into steaming basket. Reduce heat to medium and cook covered 7-8 minutes.
3. Serve immediately with melted butter or spiced oil to dip.

SEAFOOD GUMBO

This deliciously rich meal is easy to make in a slow cooker – just be careful not to overcook the seafood. Browning the vegetables first may seem unnecessary, but helps release much richer flavours.

Ingredients:

1/2 cup	Olive oil	125ml
3 cloves	Garlic, whole	3 cloves
1 medium	Onion, chopped	1 medium
3 stalks	Celery, chopped	3 stalks
12-15	Shrimp, raw	12-15
1/2 lb	Crawfish tails	250g
5-10	Scallops, raw	5-10
1 dozen	Mussels, raw	1 dozen
1 cup	Chicken broth	250ml
1 jar	Fire roasted red peppers	1 jar
1 tbsp	*Worcester sauce**	15ml
1 tsp	Cayenne pepper	5ml
1/2 tsp	Pepper	2.5ml
2	Bay leaves	2
1 tsp	Thyme	5ml
1 tsp	Basil	5ml
1 tsp	Oregano	5ml
1 tsp	Parsley, dry	5ml
1/2 tsp	Sage	2.5ml
2 tbsp	Tapioca starch, dissolved	30ml

Worcester sauce is not gluten-free. Substitute with 1 tsp (5ml) each of wheat-free tamari, molasses and vinegar/lemon juice for a strictly gluten-free version.

Instructions:

1. In a saucepan, heat oil, garlic, onion and celery over medium heat, stirring until tender.
2. Purée fire roasted red peppers (including liquid) until smooth.
3. Place seafood into slow cooker, followed by vegetables, purée, and spices. Cook on low for 4-6 hours.
4. Turn slow cooker to high and stir in tapioca starch to thicken.

Substitutions:

- Substitute individual seafood items for a large bag of frozen mixed seafood that you can find at your grocery store. Hint: crawfish tails are what give this dish a bold flavour.
- Substitute fire roasted pepper purée for 2 cups tomato pasta sauce or 2 fresh tomatoes.
- Don't fret if you're missing a couple spices, just use what you have.
- Try serving over pasta or quinoa instead of rice.

CRAB CAKES

Crab cakes are a popular appetizer you'll find at most seafood restaurants. Here's a wheat-free version that's so tasty, you might even enjoy this as a light meal on its own.

Ingredients:

1 tsp	Grapeseed oil	5ml
1 stalk	Celery, finely diced	1 stalk
1 small	Onion, finely diced	1 small
1 tbsp	Fresh parley, chopped	15ml
2	Eggs	2
1 cup	Cooked brown rice	250ml
1 tsp	Wheat-free tamari sauce	5ml
1 tsp	Molasses	5ml
1/2 tsp	Vinegar OR lemon juice	2.5ml
1 tsp	Dry mustard	5ml
1/2 tsp	Sea salt	2.5ml
12 oz	Flaked crabmeat, canned, rinsed, drained	340g

Instructions:

1. In a large frying pan, heat oil over medium heat. Add celery, onion and parsley, stirring 5 minutes until tender.
2. As vegetables are cooking, crack eggs into a medium mixing bowl. Beat until smooth. Mix in remaining ingredients.
3. Add cooked vegetables to egg and rice mixture. Add crabmeat and mix well.
4. Heat a generously oiled large frying over medium heat.
5. Form crab mixture into patties by pressing into a 1/3 cup (185ml) measuring cup. Lightly squeeze out excess liquid, leaving patties moist. Tap patty out into frying pan, and press down gently to ensure good contact with the cooking surface. Repeat, leaving space between patties.
6. Fry patties 1-2 minutes per side until cooked through and browned.
7. Serve alone, with mayonnaise, or with hummus to dip.

GARLIC SHRIMP

If you keep a bag of frozen raw shrimp in your freezer, this is a really easy dish to prepare. Shrimps cook very quickly, so be sure to watch them carefully as they will dry out easily if overcooked. Enjoy shrimp in moderation as these creatures are dwindling in numbers.

Ingredients:

1 tbsp	Butter	15ml
2 cloves	Garlic, pressed	2 cloves
12-15	Shrimp, frozen, raw	12-15
1 tsp	Water	5ml

Instructions:

1. Melt butter in large frying pan over medium heat.
2. Add garlic, stirring 1 minute until it releases its aroma.
3. Add shrimp and distribute evenly. Pour in water and cover quickly. Cook 1 minute or until under-sides turn pink. Flip shrimp over and cook covered another minute until remaining side turns pink.
4. Using a slotted spoon, scoop out individual shrimp as they finish cooking. Shrimp should be completely pink.
5. When finished, continue cooking remaining saucepan juices 1-2 minutes until thickened. Pour thickened sauce over shrimp and serve.

Substitutions:

- Substitute scallops for all or part of shrimp to add a sweet flavour to your dish.

Tip:

- Shell-on shrimp tend to be more flavourful than shelled shrimp

Herbed Pizza Crust

This is my favourite recipe for pizza crust. Because it's yeast-free, the crust is crunchy and is also much easier and less time consuming to make. You can easily double this recipe and make extra crusts to freeze for later. The next time you're craving pizza, it will be as convenient to make as having store bought crusts. Cooked and sliced crust can also double as savoury crackers for an afternoon snack.

Ingredients:

3 cups	Brown rice flour	750ml
1 cup	Tapioca starch	250ml
1-1/2 tsp	Baking powder	7.5ml
1/2 tsp	Sea salt	2.5ml
1/2 tsp	Pepper	2.5ml
1 tsp	Oregano	5ml
2 tsp	Garlic powder	10ml
1/4 cup	Grapeseed or olive oil	65ml
1-1/4 cups	Water	315ml

Instructions:

1. In a large bowl, combine all dry ingredients.
2. Blend with an electric beater on low and gradually pour in oil.
3. Add water gradually while beating. Dough should stick together easily, but should not stick easily to hands. If the dough is not sticky enough, add more water; if too sticky, add more flour.
4. Lightly grease a cookie sheet or pizza pan. Place half the dough across the centre of the pan lengthwise. Roll flat with a rolling pin to 1/4 inch thickness, or flatten with your palms. Remove excess dough from edges, and add more dough where needed until it is spread evenly and thinly across the pan. Make a second crust out of remaining dough, or refrigerate for later.
5. Bake at 350°F (175°C) for 10 minutes, or until surface appears dry. Add 5 minutes if baking from frozen.
6. If storing for later, roll dough out onto a long piece of plastic wrap in desired shape and size. Seal with plastic wrap. Place one sheet of wax paper and a piece of cardboard between each crust to ensure they freeze flat and separate easily.

PROSCIUTTO GOAT CHEESE PIZZA

I prefer to use spiced oil on my pizzas instead of tomato paste because it doesn't dominate the flavour of the pizza and the other toppings. For those of you avoiding nightshade plants, this is also a great alternative. As with any pizza, your topping combinations are almost endless!

Ingredients:

1	Pizza crust (previous recipe)	1
1 tbsp	Spiced oil	15ml
1 cup	Goat mozzarella cheese, grated	250ml
2	Green onions, sliced thinly	2
1/2 cup	Oyster mushrooms, sliced	125ml
4 slices	Prosciutto, torn to small pieces	4 slices
1/4 cup	Cilantro, chopped finely	65ml

Instructions:
1. Prepare and cook pizza crust.
2. Remove crust from oven and brush with spiced oil. Top with remaining ingredients.
3. Return pizza to oven at 350°F (175°C) for 8-10 minutes or until cheese is melted. Broil for an additional 2 minutes if desired.
4. Remove from oven, slice and serve.

Substitutions:
- You can use any kind of herb infused oil as your sauce.
- Substitute pizza oil with tomato paste if desired.
- Substitute goat mozzarella with crumbled goat feta, sheep cheese or any other allowable cheese.
- Substitute oyster mushrooms with white or brown capped mushrooms or fresh shitake mushrooms.
- Add sliced olives or red onion for extra flavour.
- Substitute prosciutto for anchovies, grilled chicken, or bacon.

ROASTED TOMATO PASTA SAUCE

Tomato sauce is so easy to make and to store that it's almost a shame to pay so much for it off the shelf. Cheap store versions are often loaded with sugar and can also contain dairy, while more "natural" sugar-free versions can be pricey. You can use any type of tomato for this recipe, but plum tomatoes are most commonly used.

Ingredients:

4	Tomatoes	4
4 cloves	Garlic, peeled, halved	4 cloves
2 tbsp	Olive oil	30ml
1 tsp	Oregano	5ml
1 tsp	Basil	5ml
	Sea salt and pepper to taste	

Instructions:

1. Rinse tomatoes and slice vertically into 2-3 sections. Remove and discard seeds if desired. Spread tomato slices and garlic evenly over a cookie sheet. Drizzle with olive oil.
2. Bake at 350°F (175°C) for 20 minutes until tomatoes pucker and centres appear dried.
3. Purée roasted tomatoes and garlic sauce in a blender. Add spices.
4. Transfer to pot and bring to boil, stirring frequently.
5. Serve immediately or store in glass jars up to 1 week or frozen up to 3 months. (Leave plenty of air space if freezing in glass jars as water will expand and can burst the glass.)

Substituions:

- For plain tomato sauce, simply omit oregano and basil.
- Try seasoning with sage, thyme or bay leaf. You can also add sautéed mushrooms, sliced black olives, capers or meatballs.

GREEN PESTO

Green pesto is the easiest and fastest pasta dressing to make from scratch. You can spice it any way you like, and all you need are three fresh ingredients – garlic, onion and parsley.

Ingredients:

3 tbsp	Olive oil	45ml
3 cloves	Garlic, pressed or minced	3 cloves
1 small	Onion, finely chopped	1 small
1 tsp	Basil	5ml
1 tsp	Oregano	5ml
1 bunch	Parley, fresh, finely chopped	1 bunch
	Sea salt and pepper to taste	

Instructions:

1. Heat oil in saucepan over medium heat.
2. Add garlic, stirring until it releases its aroma, approximately 1 minute. Stir in onion, basil and oregano. Cook covered 2-3 minutes until onion just begins to brown.
3. Stir in parsley and continue cooking, uncovered, 1-2 minutes until parsley is soft. Add sea salt and pepper to taste.
4. Toss with cooked pasta, approximately 1 tsp pesto per cup of pasta.

Substitutions:

- For different flavours, add a handful of chopped cilantro or mushrooms.
- For extra spice, try adding a fresh chopped jalapeno pepper to step 2.
- If tolerated, add goat parmesan or other cheese of choice.
- Substitute onion with shallots for a sweeter flavour.

Lasagne

This is an easy dish to make ahead of time and freeze for later. Since you are cooking the meat through before baking the entire lasagne, you can also assemble the dish one or two days ahead of time, and bake it just before you're ready to serve.

Ingredients:

1 package	Gluten-free lasagne noodles	1 package
1 tsp	Grapeseed oil	5ml
2 medium	Onions, finely diced	2 medium
1 lb	Ground turkey	500g
1 tsp	Oregano	5ml
1 tsp	Garlic powder	5ml
3 stems	Kale, finely chopped	3 stems
7-8	Oyster mushrooms, sliced	7-8
1 jar	Tomato pasta sauce	1 jar
2 cups	Goat mozzarella cheese, grated	500ml

Instructions:

1. Bring a large pot of water to a boil. Add lasagne noodles and reduce heat to medium low. Cook noodles to soften them, but not enough to cook completely. Drain, add back a small amount of cold water and set aside.
2. Heat oil in a large frying pan over medium heat. Add onions, stirring occasionally until transparent. Remove half of the cooked onions and set aside.
3. Add ground turkey and spices to frying pan with remaining onions, breaking meat apart with wooden spoon and stirring frequently to brown. Drain away excess liquid.
4. Heat a separate saucepan over medium heat and add reserved onions, kale and mushrooms. Cover, stirring occasionally 2-3 minutes until mushrooms are tender. Drain excess liquid and set aside.
5. Assemble the lasagne in layers: sauce, noodles, meat and cheese, sauce, noodles, vegetables, sauce, noodles and sauce.
6. Bake lasagne in oven at 350°F (175°C) for 30 minutes. Remove, let stand 5 minutes and serve.

Substitutions

- Substitute ground turkey with any ground meat of your choice – pork, beef, chicken or lamb.
- For a vegetarian version, substitute meat with chopped firm tofu.
- Substitute kale with spinach, arugula or other leafy greens.
- Substitute oyster mushrooms with white, brown, portobello or shitake mushrooms.

RISOTTO

This is a wonderfully creamy and rich risotto. I've never seen brown rice risotto at any restaurants, so a bonus for this recipe is its added nutrient and fibre content. This dish makes a great accompaniment to virtually any entrée.

Ingredients:

4 cups	Chicken broth	1L
1/4 cup	Onion, finely chopped	125ml
1 tbsp	Olive oil	15ml
1 cup	Brown rice	250ml
1/4 cup	Dry white wine (optional)	65ml
3 tbsp	Goat parmesan, finely grated (optional)	45ml
Pinch	Ground pepper	Pinch

Instructions:

1. In medium saucepan, bring broth to a boil.
2. In separate saucepan, cook onion with oil until tender. Stir in rice, cook 1 minute. Add wine and cook until almost evaporated.
3. Add 1/2 cup (125ml) broth to rice. Cook until liquid is absorbed, stirring frequently. Continue adding and boiling down broth 1/2 cup (125ml) at a time. (Adding it slowly like this is what makes the rice creamy.)
4. Remove from heat, add cheese and pepper. Serve immediately.

Substitutions:

- Since the goat cheese is for flavour and not for texture, you can easily omit the cheese to make a dairy-free version without sacrificing the creaminess of the risotto.

QUICHE

Making quiche is very much like making pizza – the combinations are endless. The recipe below is a very simple broccoli, cheese and bacon version. See the substitutions list below for additional suggestions.

Ingredients:

1	Pizza crust (see recipe on page 136)	1
2 tbsp	Olive oil	30ml
1	Onion, finely diced	1
1 clove	Garlic, minced	1 clove
2 cups	Broccoli, chopped to small pieces	500ml
5 slices	Bacon, cooked, diced	5 slices
1-1/2 cups	Goat mozzarella, grated	375ml
4	Eggs, beaten	4
1-1/2 cups	Soy milk or other substitute	375ml
	Sea salt and pepper to taste	

Instructions:

1. Prepare pizza crust dough. Lightly grease a 9 inch pie plate. Roll out pizza dough over wax paper to 1/4 inch thickness. Invert dough over pie plate and carefully peel away wax paper. Gently press dough into plate and trim away excess dough from edges.
2. Bake in oven at 350°F (175°C) for approximately 10-15 minutes until crisp.
3. While crust is cooking, heat oil in a large saucepan over medium-low heat. Add onions and garlic, stirring until fragrant, approximately 1 minute. Add broccoli, stirring occasionally until the vegetables are soft. Scoop vegetables into cooked crust, add bacon and sprinkle with cheese.
4. Whisk eggs and milk until well combined and smooth. Add salt and pepper. Pour egg mixture over vegetables and cheese.
5. Return to oven and continue cooking 20-30 minutes, or until center has set.

TOFU HOTPOT

This is a tasty, protein rich vegetarian dish, wonderful for a cold winter evening. The mushrooms, broth, ginger and garlic infuse a rich flavour into otherwise bland tofu. Serve this dish in large bowls with chopsticks and a spoon.

Ingredients:

2 tsp	Peanut oil OR grapeseed oil	10ml
2 tbsp	Fresh ginger, grated	30ml
6 cloves	Garlic, minced	6 cloves
2 cups	Shitake mushrooms, sliced	500ml
1 tsp	Honey	5ml
4 cups	Vegetable broth (see recipe on page 69)	1L
1/4 cup	Wheat-free tamari sauce	65ml
1 block	Firm tofu, cut in 1 inch cubes	1 block
4 stems	Bok choy, sliced thinly	4 stems
1/2 lb	Dried rice noodles	220g
1/2 cup	Fresh cilantro, chopped	125ml
2 stems	Green onion, sliced thinly	2 stems

Instructions:
1. Heat oil in large saucepan. Add ginger and garlic, cook approximately 1 minute. Add mushrooms, cooking until soft, approximately 2-3 minutes.
2. Stir in honey, broth and tamari. Cover and bring to a boil.
3. Add tofu and bok choy. Cover and simmer 2 minutes until bok choy is tender.
4. Raise heat to high. Add noodles, cook covered for about 2-3 minutes until noodles are hydrated and tender.
5. Remove from heat. Stir in cilantro and green onions and serve.

Substitutions:
- Substitute vegetable broth with chicken broth.
- Add 2 tbsp (30ml) chili paste in step 2 for a spicy version.
- Substitute rice noodles with buckwheat soba noodles or cooked brown rice.
- Substitute baby bok choy with green beans.

SNACKS AND DESERTS

Baking is where your substitution skills will come most into play. These goodies are wonderful rewards for your commitment to a healthier lifestyle.

BASIC SPONGE CAKE 146

CHOCOLATE CAKE..147

COCONUT CAKE 148

LEMON CUPCAKES..149

BUTTERCREME FROSTING 150

RAISIN BREAD 151

COCONUT LEMON MINI-LOAVES..152

CARROT CAKE 153

ZUCCHINI BREAD 154

SNACK BARS 155

SEED AND NUT COOKIES..156

ALMOND HONEY COOKIES 157

GINGERBREAD CUT-OUT COOKIES 158

CAROB CHIP COOKIES 160

TAPIOCA PUDDING..161

SWEET SOUP 162

BASIC SPONGE CAKE

This is the simplest cake recipe in this book. It is light and fluffy and very straight forward to make. Unfortunately, this cake does not store well, so make it on the same day you plan to enjoy it.

Ingredients:

6	Eggs	6
1/8 tsp	Stevia powder	0.5ml
1/2 cup	Maple syrup	125ml
1/2 cup	Brown rice flour, sifted	125ml
1/2 cup	Sweet rice flour, sifted	125ml
1 tbsp	Baking powder	15ml
8 tsp	Boiling water	40ml

Instructions:
1. Preheat oven to 350°F (175°C) and line a 6 inch cake pan with parchment paper.
2. Beat eggs with an electric beater until thick and pale, approximately 5 minutes.
3. Gradually add stevia and maple syrup and beat well.
4. Using a silicone spatula or metal spoon, fold in sifted flour and boiling water.
5. Pour batter into prepared cake pan. Bake 25 minutes, or until a skewer inserted into the centre comes out clean.

CHOCOLATE CAKE

This is my most popular cake by far. Plain or frosted, this rich chocolate cake is sure to delight with its moist, fluffy and rich, but not too sweet character. When preparing this recipe, I usually wear a dust mask to keep from inhaling flour particles, especially when sifting.

Ingredients:

6	Eggs	6
3/4 cup	Grapeseed oil	185ml
1/2 cup	Maple syrup	125ml
1/8 tsp	Stevia	0.5ml
5 tsp	Vanilla extract	25ml
2 cups	Brown rice flour	500ml
1-1/2 cup	Sweet rice flour	375ml
1 tbsp	Baking soda	15ml
3/4 cup	Cocoa	185ml
2 cups	Almond milk	500ml

Instructions:

1. Preheat oven to 350°F (175°C) and line an 8 inch cake pan with parchment paper.
2. Beat eggs with an electric beater until thick and pale, approximately 5 minutes.
3. Gradually add oil, maple syrup, stevia and vanilla, beating well after each addition.
4. Sift flours, baking soda and cocoa.
5. Add in small amount of flour mixture to wet ingredients and mix well. Mix in small amount of almond milk. Continue adding and mixing flours and almond milk alternately until all ingredients are blended together.
6. Bake for approximately 1.5 hours, or until a skewer inserted into the centre comes out clean.
7. Remove from oven and cool before frosting (optional).

COCONUT CAKE

Look for sulphite-free shredded coconut, and be sure to read ingredient labels carefully (some coconut products have added dairy). High quality coconut milk will be thick and will only contain coconut and water. If you prefer to avoid cans, you can find creamed coconut (generally sulphite-free) packed in wax paper and boxes. Creamed coconut can simply be dissolved in hot water to make coconut milk.

Ingredients:

1 cup	Butter, softened	250ml
1-1/4 cups	Xylitol	315ml
1 tsp	Coconut essence (optional)	5ml
3	Eggs	3
1 cup	Shredded coconut	250ml
1-1/2 cup	Brown rice flour	375ml
1-1/2 cup	Sweet rice flour	375ml
1 tbsp	Baking powder	15ml
1-1/4 cups	Coconut milk	315ml

Instructions:
1. Preheat oven to 350°F (175°C) and line an 8 inch cake pan.
2. Beat butter until smooth and creamy. Add xylitol and coconut essence and continue beating until fluffy. Beat in eggs.
3. Sift flours and baking powder together. Mix in shredded coconut. Fold in dry ingredients into wet ingredients alternately with spoonfuls of coconut milk.
4. Spoon batter into prepared cake pan and bake approximately 1.5 hours, or until a skewer inserted into the centre comes out clean.

Substitutions:
- Substitute butter with 3/4 cup (185ml) grapeseed oil and 1/2 cup (125ml) of additional brown rice flour.
- Substitute xylitol with 1/2 cup (125ml) maple syrup, 1/8 tsp (1ml) stevia and an extra 1/2 cup (125ml) of brown rice flour.
- For an added zing, substitute 1/4 cup (65ml) of coconut milk with 1/4 cup (65ml) freshly squeezed lemon juice, and sprinkle grated zest over the batter before cooking.

LEMON CUPCAKES

These moist cupcakes make a great substitute for a cake. Arrange them on tiered cake stands for an impressive display, or simply serve on a large plate. Serve plain or frosted, and for a special touch, top each with a fresh raspberry.

Ingredients:

5	Eggs	5
1-1/4 cups	Grapeseed oil	315ml
2 tbsp	Vanilla extract	30ml
1/2 cup	Maple syrup	125ml
1/4 tsp	Stevia powder	1ml
1/2 cup	Lemon juice	125ml
2 tsp	Baking soda	10ml
2 tsp	Baking powder	10ml
2-1/2 cups	Brown rice flour	625ml
2 cups	Sweet rice flour	500ml
1-1/2 cups	Rice milk or other substitute	375ml

Instructions:

1. Preheat oven to 350°F (175°C). Line cupcake tray with large paper liners.
2. Beat eggs with electric beater until thick and pale, approximately 5 minutes.
3. Gradually mix in oil, vanilla, maple, stevia and lemon juice.
4. In separate bowl, sift baking soda, baking powder and flours.
5. Add flour mixture to wet ingredients alternately with spoonfuls of rice milk until all ingredients are well combined.
6. Scoop batter into cupcake liners, filling 3/4 full.
7. Bake for approximately 20-25 minutes, or until skewer inserted into centre comes out clean.

Substitutions:

- Add 1/2 cup (125ml) shredded coconut for lemon coconut cupcakes.

BUTTERCRÈME FROSTING

This is a basic buttercrème frosting recipe. For richness in flavour, I usually mix butter with plain soy vegetable shortening (not margarine). If you can't tolerate dairy, table sugar, or would like to make other flavours, see the substitutions listing below.

Ingredients:

1/4 cup	Butter, room temperature	65ml
1/4 cup	Vegetable shortening	65ml
4-1/2 cups	Icing sugar, sifted	1.125L
1/4 cup	Rice milk OR water	65ml
1 tsp	Vanilla extract	5ml

Instructions:

1. Beat butter and shortening with electric mixer until fluffy. Add half icing sugar and beat well until texture becomes light and fluffy.
2. Reduce speed to low, add rice milk and vanilla.
3. Add remaining sugar, beat until fluffy, approximately 3-5 minutes. Add more water or sugar to adjust texture if needed.

Substitutions:

- For a dairy-free version, use vegetable shortening only.
- Substitute icing sugar with 4-1/2 cups (1.125L) xylitol and 4 tbsp (60ml) tapioca starch or arrowroot flour. Pulse together in blender until it becomes a fine powder.
- Mint frosting: substitute vanilla with mint extract.
- Chocolate frosting: substitute 1 cup (125ml) sugar with 1 cup cocoa powder.
- Mocha frosting: same as chocolate frosting, plus 3 tbsp instant coffee dissolved in water.
- Lemon frosting: substitute rice milk with lemon juice. Add grated rind if desired.
- Berry frosting: substitute rice milk with berry juice of choice.

RAISIN BREAD

Toast a slice of this loaf and enjoy it as a breakfast bread with butter or jam. You can also enjoy it with fresh fruit, or fried as French toast. Look for organic raisins if possible.

Ingredients:

2	Eggs	2
1/4 cup	Rice milk or substitute	65ml
1/4 cup	Maple syrup	65ml
1/4 cup	Grapeseed oil	65ml
3/4 cup	Brown rice flour	185ml
3/4 cup	Sweet rice flour	185ml
2 tsp	Baking powder	10ml
1 cup	Raisins	250ml

Instructions:

1. Preheat oven to 350°F (175°C). Lightly grease a bread pan, and sprinkle with brown rice flour to coat.
2. Beat eggs with electric beater until thick and pale. Reduce speed to low and gradually add remaining wet ingredients.
3. In separate bowl, sift flours and baking powder.
4. Combine wet and dry ingredients and mix well. Stir in raisins.
5. Scoop batter into prepared pan and bake 50 minutes or until skewer inserted into centre comes out clean.

Substitutions:

- Add 1/2 cup (125ml) walnuts or pecans for extra texture.

COCONUT LEMON MINI-LOAVES

These coconut lemon mini-loaves makes a great dessert to finish a good meal. Pack leftovers with your lunch for an afternoon snack, or enjoy it for midnight munchies.

Ingredients:

4	Eggs	4
1-1/2 cups	Rice milk	375ml
1 cup	Maple syrup	250ml
1/2 cup	Grapeseed oil	125ml
1/2 cup	Lemon juice and grated rind	125ml
2 cups	Brown rice flour	500ml
1-1/2 cups	Sweet rice flour	375ml
4 tsp	Baking powder	20ml
1 cup	Shredded coconut	250ml

Instructions:
1. Preheat oven to 350°F (175°C). Lightly grease a mini-loaf tray, and sprinkle with brown rice flour to coat.
2. In a large bowl, beat eggs until pale and thick. Mix in remaining wet ingredients including lemon rind, reserving 1 tbsp lemon juice.
3. In separate bowl, sift together flours and baking powder and stir in shredded coconut. Add wet ingredients to dry ingredients and mix well.
4. Pour batter into a prepared mini-loaf tray. Bake for 30-40 minutes, or until tops brown and an inserted toothpick comes out clean.
5. Remove from oven and brush tops with reserved lemon juice. Once cool, slice and serve. Store in an airtight container on the countertop or in the fridge.

Substitutions:
- Substitute maple syrup with stevia and/or honey.
- If you don't have a mini-loaf tray, you can make these into cupcakes as well.

CARROT CAKE

Carrot cake is a great way to sneak in vegetables into your day. This dense cake will store well for several days and can even be wrapped and frozen for later.

Ingredients:

3	Eggs	3
1/2 cup	Grapeseed oil	125ml
1/4 cup	Maple syrup	65ml
1/4 tsp	Stevia powder	1ml
1 cup	Brown rice flour	250ml
1 cup	Sweet rice flour	250ml
1/2 tsp	Baking soda	2.5ml
1 tsp	Cinnamon	5ml
1 tsp	Ground ginger	5ml
1-1/4 cups	Carrot, finely grated	315ml
1/2 cup	Raisins	125ml
1/2 cup	Pecans, crushed	125ml

Instructions:

1. Preheat oven to 350°F (175°C). Lightly grease a bread pan, and sprinkle with brown rice flour to coat. You can also prepare these as cupcakes in a lined cupcake baking tray.
2. Beat eggs until smooth. Mix in oil, maple syrup and stevia.
3. In separate bowl, sift flours, baking soda and spices. Pour wet ingredients into dry and stir until combined.
4. Stir in carrot, raisins and pecans.
5. Spoon into loaf pan or cupcake tray.
6. Bake until a skewer inserted into the centre comes out clean, approximately 1-1/2 hours (20-30 minutes for cupcakes).

Substitutions:

- Substitute pecans with walnuts.
- Add 1/4 tsp (1ml) nutmeg for more zing.

ZUCCHINI BREAD

Zucchini bread is a great way to use up extra quantities of this boun-
tiful squash when it comes into season in the fall. This bread is surprisingly moist and makes a great mid-day snack.

Ingredients:

1	Egg	1
1/4 cup	Grapeseed oil	65ml
1/4 cup	Maple syrup OR honey	65ml
2 cups	Zucchini, grated	500ml
3/4 cup	Brown rice four	185ml
3/4 cup	Sweet rice flour	185ml
1 tsp	Baking powder	5ml
1/2 tsp	Baking soda	2.5ml
1 tsp	Cinnamon	5ml
1/2 tsp	Sea salt	2.5ml
1/2 cup	Walnuts, chopped	125ml

Instructions:

1. Preheat oven to 350°F (175°C). Lightly grease a bread pan, and
   sprinkle with brown rice flour to coat.
2. In a large bowl, beat egg and add remaining wet ingredients including zucchini.
3. In a separate bowl, mix dry ingredients. Combine dry and wet
   ingredients.
4. Pour batter into prepared pan and bake for 60 minutes, or until a
   skewer inserted in the middle comes out clean.
5. Remove from oven and cool for 5 minutes before turning out of
   pan.

SNACK BARS

A nutty alternative to granola bars – these high protein snacks are tasty, convenient and easy to make.

Ingredients:

1 cup	Almonds, roughly chopped	250ml
1 cup	Walnuts, crushed	250ml
1 cup	Pecans, crushed	250ml
1/2 cup	Pine nuts	125ml
1/2 cup	Sesame seeds	125ml
1 cup	Honey OR brown rice syrup	250ml

Instructions:
1. Preheat oven to 350°F (175°C). Lightly grease a cookie sheet and set aside. If using brown rice syrup, you may want to line the cookie sheet with parchment paper instead of greasing it.
2. Mix nuts together in a large bowl and combine with honey.
3. Scoop nuts onto cookie sheet and spread evenly, pressing down to eliminate as much air as possible. (You may lightly oil hands to keep nuts from sticking to you.)
4. Bake for 5 minutes until honey begins to harden.
5. Slice with a sharp knife or pizza cutter and remove from cookie sheet while still warm. Once cool, store in a reusable container or wrap individually in wax paper or plastic wrap.

SEED AND NUT COOKIES

These are filling cookies and make a great afternoon snack. These are best made as small bite sized cookies as they can be a little messy to eat. The cookies will be very sticky, so they're best cooked on top of a parchment lined cookie sheet.

Ingredients:

2 cups	Brown rice flakes	500ml
3/4 cup	Brown rice flour	185ml
1/4 cup	Tapioca starch	65ml
3/4 cup	Sesame seeds	185ml
1 cup	Sunflower Seeds	250ml
1/2 cup	Flax seeds	125ml
1/2 cup	Almonds, slivered or sliced	125ml
1/2 cup	Grapeseed oil	125ml
1/2 cup	Rice syrup	125ml
1/2 cup	Honey	125ml
1/3 cup	Tahini	85ml
1/2 cup	Rice milk	125ml

Instructions:
1. Preheat oven to 350°F (175°C). Line a cookie sheet with parchment paper.
2. In a large bowl, mix together dry ingredients.
3. In a separate bowl, mix together wet ingredients. Pour wet ingredients into dry and combine.
4. Drop batter by the spoonful onto paper and flatten cookies to 1/3 inch (1cm) thickness.
5. Bake 350°F (175°C) for 20-25 minutes until edges turn brown.

Substitutions:
- You can use any combination of seeds and nuts, as long the total quantity adds up to approximately 3 cups (750ml). Try pecans, cashews, walnuts, pumpkin seeds or hulled hemp seeds.
- For a slightly different taste, substitute rice milk with apple or pear juice.

ALMOND HONEY COOKIES

Here's a variation on the classic peanut butter cookie. This recipe yields approximately 6 dozen bite sized cookies. If this is too much, simply freeze leftover dough in plastic wrap for later. The dough may feel slightly oily to the touch, but once cooked, will yield a great cookie.

Ingredients:

2	Eggs	2
3/4 cup	Grapeseed oil	185ml
1 cup	Almond butter	250ml
1 cup	Honey	250ml
2-1/2 cups	Brown rice flour	625ml
1-1/2 cups	Tapioca starch	375ml
2 tsp	Baking soda	10ml

Instructions:
1. Preheat oven to 350°F (175°C).
2. Mix oil, almond butter, honey and egg well in a medium mixing bowl.
3. Add flours and baking soda, mix well.
4. Using a heaping tablespoon of batter per cookie, form into balls on baking sheet, 1 inch apart.
5. Press cookies twice at right angles with a fork to make a grid pattern.
6. Bake for approximately 12 minutes or until edges begin to brown.

GINGERBREAD CUT-OUT COOKIES

The smell of these gingerbread cookies are so familiar, they might make you forget about the fact that they're gluten-free. A few inexpensive cookie cutters make this a fun activity and a fun snack.

Ingredients:

2-1/2 cups	Brown rice flour	625ml
1 cup	Tapioca starch	250ml
2 tsp	Ginger, ground	10ml
2 tsp	Cinnamon, ground	10ml
1/4 tsp	Nutmeg, ground	1ml
1/4 tsp	Dry mustard	1ml
1/8 tsp	Cloves, ground	0.5ml
1 tsp	Baking soda	5ml
1/2 tsp	Sea salt	2.5ml
1/4 tsp	Allspice	1ml
1 cup	Butter, softened	250ml
1/2 cup	Molasses	125ml
1	Egg	1
1/2 tsp	Vanilla extract	2.5ml
1/4 cup	Maple syrup	65ml

Instructions:
1. Preheat oven to 350°F (175°C).
2. Combine all dry ingredients in a large bowl.
3. In separate bowl, beat butter with an electric mixer until smooth. Reduce speed to low and gradually beat in molasses, egg, vanilla and maple syrup.
4. Gradually add dry ingredients, beating well. Dough should be tacky but not overly sticky. If dough seems too moist and sticky, you may add up to 1/2 cup (125ml) more tapioca starch to achieve desired texture.
5. Form dough into balls, wrap in plastic wrap and refrigerate 4 hours or overnight.

6. Prepare clean counter by covering with a sheet of wax paper. Unwrap chilled dough and place over wax paper. Flatten dough with the palm of your hand to 1 inch thickness. (You may lightly oil your hands to keep dough from sticking).
7. Place a second sheet of wax paper over the flattened dough. Use a rolling pin to roll dough to 1/4 inch thickness throughout.
8. Gently peel away top sheet of wax paper. Cut out shapes with cookie cutters. If dough becomes too sticky or soft to handle, return to refrigerator for 10-20 minutes before continuing.
9. Transfer cookies to baking sheet and bake for 8-12 minutes until edges begin to darken.

Substitutions:

- For a dairy-free version, substitute butter with 3/4 cup grapeseed oil and an extra 1/2 cup of tapioca starch

CAROB CHIP COOKIES

Here's a twist on the classic chocolate chip cookie. If you can't tolerate cocoa, this is a great alternative. Be sure to read carob chip ingredient labels carefully, as some may contain gluten (malt) or dairy.

Ingredients:

2	Eggs	2
1/3 cup	Grapeseed oil	85ml
1/2 cup	Honey	125ml
1 tsp	Vanilla extract	5ml
1-1/2 cups	Brown rice flour	375ml
3/4 cup	Tapioca starch	185ml
2 tsp	Baking powder	10ml
1/4 tsp	Sea salt	1ml
2 cups	Carob chips	500ml

Instructions:
1. Preheat oven to 350°F (175°C) and lightly grease a cookie sheet.
2. Beat eggs and mix well with oil, honey and vanilla.
3. In a separate bowl, sift together flours, baking powder and salt.
4. Combine wet and dry ingredients and mix well. Stir in carob chips.
5. Drop by the tablespoon onto prepared cookie sheet and bake 10 minutes or until cooked as desired.

TAPIOCA PUDDING

Tapioca pudding is much like rice pudding. It's very easy to make, but does require being soaked overnight before cooking. Tapioca pearls are easily found in Asian supermarkets, and are sometimes carried in the ethnic food aisle at your local grocery store.

Ingredients:

1/2 cup	Tapioca pearls	125ml
3 cups	Rice or coconut milk	750ml
1/4 cup	Maple syrup	65ml
2	Eggs, well beaten	2

Instructions:

1. Soak tapioca pearls overnight in a medium bowl of water.
2. Drain tapioca and pour into top of double boiler. If you don't have a double boiler, you can simply place a small pot inside a larger pot. Fill the bottom pot with water, and fill the top pot with the recipe ingredients.
3. Add milk, maple syrup and eggs. Stir gently to combine.
4. Cook over medium heat approximately 15 minutes stirring occasionally. Pudding is done when pearls are mostly translucent and pudding is thick.
5. Remove from heat and cool for 30 minutes. Serve alone or with fresh fruit of your choice.

SWEET SOUP

This is a version of a commonly enjoyed Chinese sweet soup, often served as dessert. You can also enjoy this for breakfast or for an afternoon or late night snack.

Ingredients:

1 large	Sweet potato, peeled, cubed	1 large
4-6	Taro roots, peeled, cubed	4-6
2 inches	Fresh ginger, peeled, sliced	5cm
8 dried	Red Chinese dates	8 dried
2 tbsp	Honey	30ml

Instructions:
1. Fill large saucepan with water and bring to a boil. Add all ingredients to pot.
2. Reduce heat to low and simmer, covered, 30-40 minutes until root vegetables are very tender.
3. Serve hot or cold. Add more honey to taste as desired.

COOKING CONVERSIONS

TEMPERATURES

Fahrenheit (°F)	Celsius (°C)
250	120
275	135
300	150
325	165
350	175
375	190
400	205
425	220

MEASUREMENTS

Imperial	Metric
1/8 tsp	0.5ml
1/4 tsp	1ml
1/2 tsp	2.5ml
1 tsp	5ml
1 tbsp	15ml
1/3 cup	85ml
1/2 cup	125ml
1 cup	250ml
1 lb	500 g

METRIC
SUBSTITUTION CHART CONVERSIONS

GLUTEN AS A BINDING (STICKY) AID (from page 24)

Binding aid	Best for	Substitution for 250ml wheat flour
Tapioca starch (also labelled as tapioca flour)	Dense baked goods such as pizza crusts and crackers. Great for thickening sauces and gravies. Can also work well in cakes. Very similar to arrowroot flour, but much cheaper.	185ml brown rice flour 65ml tapioca starch 2.5ml baking powder
Arrowroot flour	Dense baked goods such as pizza crusts and crackers. Can also work well in cakes. Can be expensive.	185ml brown rice flour 65ml arrowroot flour 2.5ml baking powder
Arrowroot powder	Most baked goods. Can be expensive.	250ml brown rice flour 15ml arrowroot powder 2.5ml baking powder
Sweet rice flour	Delicate baked goods such as cakes, cupcakes, waffles. Yields very moist and light products.	125ml brown rice flour 125ml sweet rice flour 2.5ml baking powder
Gelatine (animal based) OR Agar flakes (algae based / vegan)	Great for thickening desserts such as custards, jams or pie fillings. I prefer not to use this for gravies as it tends to make them gelatinous instead of creamy and thick.	5ml of gelatine or agar flakes dissolved in warm water will generally thicken approximately 250ml of liquid ingredients

DAIRY SUBSTITUTIONS (from page 32)

Ingredient	Best for	Substitution for 250ml cow milk
Soy milk (look for unsweetened)	Any baked goods, cereal, coffee, drinks and smoothies	250ml soy milk
Almond milk (look for unsweetened)	Any baked goods, cereal, coffee, drinks and smoothies	250ml almond milk
Goat milk or sheep milk	Any savoury foods like pasta sauces	250ml goat or sheep milk
Rice milk (I recommend brown rice milk)	Any baked goods, cereal, coffee, drinks and smoothies.	250ml rice milk
Water	Anytime you open your cupboard and realize you've run out of milk substitutes!	250ml water

Ingredient	Best for	Substitution for 250ml butter
Grapeseed Oil	Use in place of butter in baked goods	185ml grapeseed oil
Olive Oil	Use in place of butter in savoury dishes	185ml olive oil

SUGAR SUBSTITUTIONS (from page 36)

Ingredient	Best for	Substitution for 250ml refined white sugar
Stevia*	Baked goods, drinks	1ml powdered OR 10 drops of liquid Stevia
Honey	Baked goods, drinks, smoothies, spreads	185ml unpasteurized honey
Maple syrup	Baked goods, pancakes/waffles	185ml maple syrup
Agave nectar*	Baked goods, pancakes/waffles	185ml agave nectar
Xylitol*	Baked goods, frostings	250ml xylitol
Rice syrup	Baked goods, snack bars	250ml rice syrup
Fruit juice	Baked goods, drinks, smoothies	250ml fruit juice
Molasses (related to wheat)	Gingerbread cookies, baked goods calling for brown sugar	185ml molasses

TROUBLESHOOTING GUIDE (from page 46)

Problem	Reason	Recommended fix for 20cm cake, bread loaf or 2 dozen cupcakes
Cooked on the outside and raw or soggy in the middle	Not cooked long enough; OR Too much fat content OR Baking pan is too big	Return to oven and check every 5 minutes. If middle remains soggy despite a long cooking time, there is too much fat. Cut 65-125ml oil from recipe. If problem persists, add 125ml flours as well and/or try using a smaller baking pan.
Too dry	Not enough fat content	Add 65ml cup oil, OR Add 1 egg and reduce water/milk by 250ml
Too crumbly	Not enough binding aids	Add 30ml psyllium husks and 65ml water; OR Add 1 egg and 185-250ml flour OR Add 65-125ml tapioca flour (or other binding aid), reduce bulk flour by same amount
Too tough or chewy (cake)	Too much binding aid	Reduce 65-125ml binding aid, increase bulk flour by same amount
Didn't rise enough, too dense	Not enough leavening aids	Add 15ml baking powder; AND/OR Add 1 egg and 125ml flour
Too tough or chewy (crust/crackers)	Not enough leavening aids	Add 15ml baking powder; AND/OR Add 1 egg and 185-250ml flour
Started to burn early in oven	Too much sugar content	If using maple syrup, reduce amount used and substitute honey or stevia
Caused an adverse reaction	Contamination	Check all labels carefully. Call manufacturers if in doubt. Check for and eliminate contamination sources.

BIBLIOGRAPHY

Agricultural Marketing Resource Center. "Buckwheat Profile." http://www.agmrc.org. Retrieved October 2, 2009.

Bendel CM, Wiesner SM, Garni RM, Cebelinski E and Wells CL. Department of Pediatrics, University of Minnesota, Minneapolis, Minnesota. "Cecal colonization and systemic spread of Candida albicans in mice treated with antibiotics and dexamethasone." *Pediatrric Research.* 51.3 (2002):290-295.

Crellin JK, Philpott J, and Bass ALT. *A Reference Guide to Medicinal Plants: Herbal Medicine Past and Present.* North Carolina: Duke University Press, 1989.

Dodson and Dunmire. *Mountain Wildfowers of the Southern Rockies.* New Mexico: University of New Mexico Press, 2007.

Environmental Working Group. "Shopper's Guide to Pesticides." http://www.foodnews.org. Retrieved November 29, 2009.

Garvan Institute of Medical Research. "A Ton Of Bitter Melon Produces Sweet Results For Diabetes." *ScienceDaily,* March 27, 2008.

Harris, JC; Cottrell, SL; Plummer, S and Lloyd, D. "Antimicrobial properties of Allium sativum (garlic)." *Applied Microbiology and Biotechnology.* 57.3 (2001):282–286.

Health Canada. *Infant Botulism.* http://www.hc-sc.gc.ca. Updated January 2009.

Health Canada. *Celiac Disease – The Gluten Connection.* http://www.healthcanada.gc.ca/celiac. Updated 2009.

Howard, Michael. *Traditional Folk Remedies.* London: Century, 1987.

Lynch H, and Milgrom P. "Xylitol and dental caries: an overview for clinicians." *Journal of the California Dental Association*. 31.3 (2003):205-9.

Market Analysis Group, Grains and Oilseeds Division, Food Value Chain Bureau, Market and Industry Services Branch, Agriculture & Agri-Food. "Market Outlook Report – Corn: Situation And Outlook." www.agr.gc.ca. 1.2 (2009): 3-4.

Mascolo N, Jain R, Jain S, and Capasso F. Department of Experimental Pharmacology, University of Naples, Italy. "Ethnopharmacologic investigations of ginger (Zingiber officinale)." *Journal of Ethnopharmacology*. 27.1-2 (1989):129-40.

McMillan M, Spinks EA, and Fenwick GR. "Preliminary observations on the effect of dietary brussels sprouts on thyroid function." *Human Toxicology*. 5.1 (1986): 15-19.

National Cancer Institute, U.S. National Institutes of Health. "Dictionary of Cancer Terms: sesquiterpene lactone and watercress." http://www.cancer.gov/dictionary. Retrieved November 29, 2009.

National Institute of Arthritis and Musculoskeletal and Skin Diseases. "Conditions and Behaviors that Increase Osteoporosis Risk: What People With Lactose Intolerance Need to Know About Osteoporosis." http://www.niams.nih.gov. Reviewed January 2009.

Ontario Corn Producers' Association. "A Zillion Uses for Corn." www.ontariocorn.org. Retrieved September 30, 2009.

Panel on Micronutrients, Subcommittees on Upper Reference Levels of Nutrients and of Interpretation and Use of Dietary Reference Intakes, Standing Committee on the Scientific Evaluation of Dietary Reference Intakes, Food and Nutrition Board and Institute of Medicine. *Dietary Reference Intakes for Vitamin A, Vitamin K, Arsenic, Boron, Chromium, Copper, Iodine, Iron, Manganese, Molybdenum, Nickel, Silicon, Vanadium, and Zinc.* D.C.: National Academy Press, 2001.

Quintaes KD, Farfan JA, Tomazini FM, Morgano MA, de Almeyda Hajisa NM and Neto JT. "Mineral Migration and Influence of Meal Preparation in Iron Cookware on the Iron Nutritional Status of Vegetarian Students." *Ecology of Food and Nutrition.* 46.2 (2007):125-141.

Thompson LU, Boucher BA, Liu Z, Cotterchio M, and Kreiger N. Department of Nutritional Sciences, University of Toronto. "Phytoestrogen content of foods consumed in Canada, including isoflavones, lignans, and coumestan." *Nutrition and Cancer.* 54.2 (2006): 184-201.

Timlin MT, Pereira MA, Story M and Neumark-Sztainer D. Division of Epidemiology and Community Health, University of Minnesota and Minneapolis. "Breakfast Eating and Weight Change in a 5-Year Prospective Analysis of Adolescents: Project EAT (Eating Among Teens)." *Pediatrics.* 121.3 (2008): 638-645.

Váli L, Stefanovits-Bányai E, Szentmihályi K, Fébel H, Sárdi E, Lugasi A, Kocsis I, and Blázovics A. II Department of Medicine, Semmelweis University, Budapest, Hungary. "Liver-protecting effects of table beet (Beta vulgaris var. rubra) during ischemia-reperfusion." *Nutrition.* 23.2 (2007): 172-178.

Webb AJ, Patel N, Loukogeorgakis S, Okorie M, Aboud Z, Misra S, Rashid R, Miall P, Deanfield J, Benjamin N, MacAllister R, Hobbs AJ and Ahluwalia A. "Acute Blood Pressure Lowering, Vasoprotective, and Antiplatelet Properties of Dietary Nitrate via Bioconversion to Nitrite." *Hypertension.* 51 (2008): 784.

Weed, Susun S. *The Wise Woman Herbal: Healing Wise.* New York: Ash Tree Publishing, 1989.

Wikipedia. *List of Culinary Vegetables.* http://en.wikipedia.org/wiki/List_of_culinary_vegetables. Retrieved November 1, 2009.

Winkler C, Wirleitner B, Schroecksnadel K, Schennach H and Fuchs D. Division of Biological Chemistry, Biocentre, Innsbruck Medical University, Ludwig Boltzmann Institute of AIDS-Research, Innsbruck Central Institute of Blood Transfusion and Immunology, University Hospital. "In vitro Effects of Beet Root Juice on Stimulated and Unstimulated Peripheral Blood Mononuclear Cells." *American Journal of Biochemistry and Biotechnology*. 1.4 (2005): 180-185.

Xia, Tao, and Wang, Qin. College of Life Science, East China Normal University, Shanghai and College of Life Science and Biotechnology, Shanghai Jiaotong University, Shanghai. "Hypoglycaemic role of Cucurbita ficifolia (Cucurbitaceae) fruit extract in streptozotocin-induced diabetic rats." *Journal Of The Science Of Food And Agriculture*. 87.9 (2007): 1753-1757.

Yamahara J, Huang Q, Li Y, Xu L, and Fujimura H. Kyoto Pharmacological University, Japan. "Gastrointestinal motility enhancing effect of ginger and its active constituents." *Chemical and Pharmaceutical Bulletin*. 38.2 (1990): 430-431.

INDEX

A

Apples
  Recipes with
    Blueberry apple smoothie 80

B

Beef
  Recipes with
    Basic broth...68
    Chicken hummus salad rolls (substitute) 110
    French onion soup 72
    Lasagne (substitute).. 140
    Roast beef 125
    Venison stew (substitute) 122
Bell pepper
  Recipes with
    Chicken with cashews 117
    Seafood gumbo... 132
    Stuffed bell peppers 107
    Vegetarian okra stew..70
Binding Aids
  Arrowroot starch or flour 25
  Gelatine and Agar...25
  Sweet rice flour 25
  Tapioca starch 25
Bok Choy
  Recipes with
    Bok choy with mushrooms... 102
    Poached black cod with rice nookes and bok choy 129
    Tofu hotpot.. 144
Bread
  Recipes
    Cocount lemon mini-loaves... 152
    Quick bread..84
    Raisin bread 151
    Zucchini bread 154

Breakfast
  Recipes
    Blueberry apple smoothie 80
    Hot cereal..79
    Waffles and pancakes..78
Broccoli
  Recipes with
    Broccoli...95
    Quiche 143

C

Cakes
  Recipes
    Basic sponge cake 146
    Carrot cake.. 153
    Chocolate cake 147
    Coconut cake.. 148
    Coconut lemon mini-loaves... 152
    Lemon Cupcakes 149
    Zucchini bread 154
Chicken
  Complimentary spices..62
  Cooking temperature 11
  Recipes with
    Basic broth..68
    Chicken fried rice 116
    Chicken hummus salad rolls 110
    Chicken sandwich.. 112
    Chicken with cashews.. 117
    Hamburgers (substitute) 124
    Lasagne (substitute).. 140
    Tomato egg drop soup 74
    Vietnamese spring rolls 111
    Whole roast chicken with root vegetables.............................. 118
Cookies
  Recipes
    Almond honey cookies.. 157
    Carob chip cookies.. 160
    Gingerbread cut-out cookies 158
    Seed and nut cookies 156

D

Dairy
    Sources 30–31
    Substituting
        Almond milk 33
        Goat milk 33
        Rice milk 33
        Soy milk 32

E

Egg
    Recipes with
        Chicken fried rice 116
        Egg or tuna salad sandwich 114
        Quiche 143
        Western omelette 81

F

Fennel, recipe
    Roasted fennel 101
Fiddlehead, recipe
    Buttered fiddleheads 94
Fish
    Cooking temperature 11
    Recipes with
        Garlic butter salmon 130
        Poached black cod with rice nookes and bok choy ... 129
Food Safety
    Buyer Beware 9
    Cross Contamination 7–9
    Danger zone 10
    Fire safety 11–12
    Meat, cooking temperatures 11
Frosting, recipe
    Buttercreme frosting 150

G

Gluten and Wheat
    Sources 21–22
    Substituting - binding characteristics 23–26
    Substituting – bulk characteristics 23
    Substituting - examples 29

    Substituting - leavening characteristics 26–27
Goat Milk...33
  Recipes with
    Alternative yogurt...82
    Alternative yogurt cheese 83
Grains
  Amaranth flour 23
  Buckwheat 48
  Millet..48
    Recipes with
    Quinoa or Millet 90
  Millet flour..23
  Quinoa...48
    Recipes with
    Quinoa or Millet 90
  Quinoa flour..23
  Rice 47
    Recipes with
    Coconut steamed rice 87
    Kale with rice 100
    Risotto 142
    Saffron steamed rice...88
    Steamed rice 86
    Wild rice 89
  Rice flour 23
  Teff flour...23
  Wild rice 48
Guylan, recipe
  Guylan in garlic.. 103

K

Kale, recipe
  Kale with rice 100
Kitchen Tools
  Equipment...16
  Pantry items..13

L

Leavening Aids
  Baking powder..27
  Baking soda 26
  Cook in smaller dishes...27

Yeast 26

M

Meats
    Basic tips 62–63
    Fish tips..63
    Fish, mercury...63–64
    Wild game tips..63
Millet
    Recipes with
        Hot cereal...79
Mushrooms
    Recipes with
        Bok choy with mushrooms................................ 102
        Chili... 120
        Portobello mushrooms with porschiutto 128
        Tofu hotpot.. 144
        Western omelette..81

O

Okra
    Recipes with
        Vegetarian okra stew.......................................70

P

Pasta
    Recipes
        Green pesto 139
        Roasted tomato pasta sauce............................. 138
Pizza
    Recipes
        Herbed pizza crust 136
        Porsciuotto goat cheese pizza 137
Pork
    Complimentary spices...62
    Cooking temperature 11
    Recipes with
        Basic broth...68
        Breaded pork chops 127
        Chicken fried rice (substitute)........................... 116
        Chicken hummus salad rolls (substitute) 110
        Hamburgers (substitute) 124
        Honey-garlic bbq ribs 126

Lasagne (substitute) 140
Porsciutto goat cheese pizza 137
Portobello mushrooms with porschiutto 128
Venison stew (substitute) 122
Vietnamese spring rolls 111
Winter melon watercress soup 75

S

Salad, recipe
    Roasted almond pecan salad 92
Seafood
    Recipes with
        Buttered lobster or crab 131
        Crab cakes 134
        Garlic shrimp 135
        Seafood gumbo 132
Shrimp
    Recipes with
        Chicken hummus salad rolls (substitute) 110
        Seafood gumbo 132
        Vietnamese spring rolls 111
Snack bars, recipe 155
Snow pea, recipe
    Snow peas 99
Squash
    Recipes with
        Butternut Squash 104
        Butternut squash soup 72
        Spaghetti squash 105
        Stuffed buttercup squash 106
String bean, recipe
    String beans 98
Sugar
    basics 35
    Sources 35–36
    Substituting 36–38
Sweet potato
    Recipes with
        Sweet potato chips 97
        Sweet soup 162
Sweeteners, natural
    Agave nectar 37

Fruit juice 38
Honey 37
Maple syrup 37
Molasses 38
Rice malt 38
Xylitol 37–38

T

Tapioca
  Recipe
    Tapioca pudding 161
Time management
  Buying in bulk 16–17
  Storing in bulk 17–18
Tofu
  Recipes with
    Tofu hotpot 144
Tomato
  Recipes with
    Chili 120
    Roasted tomato pasta sauce 138
    Seafood gumbo (substitute) 132
    Stuffed bell peppers 107
    Zucchini and tomato 96
Tuna
  Recipes with
    Egg or tuna salad sandwich 114
Turkey
  Complimentary spices 62
  Cooking temperature 11
  Recipes with
    Basic broth 68
    Chicken hummus salad rolls (substitute) 110
    Chicken sandwich (substitute) 112
    Chili 120
    Lasagne 140

V

Vegetables
  Flowers and flower buds 55
  Fruits 53–54
  Leafy and salad 49–53

Podded 55–58
Root and tuberous... 58–61
Squashes and melons 54–55
Venison
    Recipes with
        Venison stew 122

Z

Zucchini, Recipes with
    Zucchini and tomato..96
    Zucchini bread 154

MY RECIPES

MY RECIPES

GIVE THE GIFT OF *WHERE DO I START?*
TO YOUR FRIENDS AND COLLEAGUES
Order direct online at www.glutenfreeliving.ca or Order Here

□ **YES**, I want _____ copies of *Where Do I Start?* for $24.95 each.
□ **YES**, I am interested in having Victoria Yeh speak or give a seminar to my company, association, school, support group or organization. Please send me information.

Canada/U.S.: Include $4.00 shipping and handling for one book, and $2.00 for each additional book. Canadian residents must add 5% GST.

Prices shown are in both U.S. and Canadian funds. Orders shipping to the U.S. must be made in U.S. funds; orders shipping to Canada must be made in Canadian funds. Payment must accompany orders. Please allow 3-5 weeks for delivery.

My cheque or money order for $_____ is enclosed
Please charge my □ Visa □ MasterCard

Name   Organization

Address

City, Prov/State, Postal/Zip

Phone (   )   E-mail

Card#

Exp Date   Signature

Make your cheque payable and return to:
Vector One Publishing
PO Box 97532, RPO Highland Creek
Scarborough, ON M1C 4Z1

Volume discounts are available.
For more information, to order online, or for International orders,
visit **www.glutenfreeliving.ca**